Eminem

THE STORIES BEHIND EVERY SONG

THIS IS A CARLTON BOOK

First published by Carlton Books Limited 2003
This revised and updated edition published in 2012 by
Carlton Books Limited
20 Mortimer Street
London W1T 3JW

Hardback ISBN 978 1 78097 004 2
Flexi ISBN 978 1 78097 157 5

Printed in China

The publishers would like to thank the following sources for their kind permission to reproduce the pictures in this book:

Corbis: Steve Azzara 56, Stephane Cardinale 8, Najlah Feanny 94, Rune Hellestad 34, 84, 85, PACHA 35, David Turnley 12 Roland Hall 27 (background)
Getty Images: Barry Brechelsen 157, Michael Caulfield Archive/Wireimage 135, C.Flanigan/FilmMagic 147 b, Dave Hogan 148 b, Samie Hussein 166, 169, Sean Gardner 146, Scott Gries 141, Yuri Gripas 136, Jeff Kravitz 159, Hector Mata/AFP 149 t, Kevin Mazur/Wireimage 4, 133, 139, 154, 159, 170 Jason Merritt/FilmMagic 160, Frank Micelotta 96, 123, Ethan Miller 134, Tim Mosenfelder 165, Johnny Nunez 149, 171, Christopher Polk/AMA2010 162, Bill Pugliano 6, 14, 20, 115, Matthew Simmons 128, Paul Warner 131, 151, Kevin Winter 144
Photos.com: Collection Cinéma 117, 118, 120, 122, 126, 127
Retna: David Atlas 81, Janette Beckman 19, Jay Blakesberg 33, Wilberto Boogaard 7, Bob Carey/LA Times 87, Andrew Carruth: 17, Jack Cousin 112, Bill Davila 42, Beatrice De Gea 60, Steven Dewall 125, Vincent Dolman 46, Kevin Estrada 58, Patrick Ford 52, Gary Friedman/LA Times 102, Armando Gallo 95, Robert Gauthier 45, 109, Steve Granitz: 40, John Hryniuk 62, JM International/ Redferns 100, 104, Sian Kennedy 49, Bernhard Kuhmstedt 57, Sam Levi 26, Jon Mather 88, 93, 107 Sly Matrix 38, Chris McAndrew 101, Brad Miller 82, Debra L. Rothenberg 64, Michael Schreiber: 23, 24, 27, 28, Nancy J. Sims 98, Ed Sirrs 50, Kelly A. Swift 10, 36, 74, Barry Talesnick 15, Niels Van Iperen 124, Brian Walski/LA Times 5, 41,Michael Wilfling/Vanit: 16, 77
Rex Features: Fotos International 55

Every effort has been made to acknowledge correctly and contact the source and/or copyright holder of each picture and Carlton Books apologises for any unintentional errors or omissions, which will be corrected in future editions of this book.

Eminem

THE STORIES BEHIND EVERY SONG

DAVID STUBBS

CONTENTS

INTRODUCTION

In the history of hip hop, rock or pop there never been anyone quite like Eminem. He hits all the buttons pushed over the years by gangsta rap, Elvis, Kurt Cobain, MTV, Jerry Springer, Howard Stern, Madonna, Tupac, Lenny Bruce, at once. Freestyling, cartoon-hilarious, beyond the pale, unrelentingly insolent, twinkling with blue-eyed charm, outrageously indiscreet, brash and yet, beneath that thin pasty skin of his, highly sensitive. He is a self-made and dope antidote to celebrity culture as well as its supreme product. He rolls across the celebscape like a drunken kid joyriding in a stolen steamroller, throwing up controversy and scandal in his wake, trampling over all the exposed tender points of modern-day American discourse – race, gender, censorship, obscenity, the Columbine massacres, the White House, America's pop sweethearts – with a fine disregard for delicate sensibilities.

But he's more than a smirking satirist. Smart but not college-smart, his private life is all part of the turmoil he exposes and thrives on. His own mother sued him, his own grandmother threatened to sue him, his wife divorced him twice. It's all part of the fun, all the same shit.

Not for nothing has he been described by Newsweek as "the most compelling figure in all of pop music". He's the last live spark in a pop world

in which the forces of marketing and manufacturing have all but sealed into the skirting boards any possibility of spontaneity and badmouth attitude. Whether you're heartened by his all-American tale of a boy who, in the face of miserable social and familial odds, captured the hearts and minds of millions, or perturbed by his nihilistic and deliberately unhelpful exposé of the miserable and messed up state of the American psyche, the fact is that this is Eminem's world and we're living in it. And, if his sale figures are anything to go by, loving it.

In a sense, Eminem "isn't really music" – or rather, listening to Eminem transcends the usual experience of listening to music. The beats and productions laid down for him by the likes of Dre and the Bass Brothers on The Slim Shady LP and The Marshall Mathers LP are often deliberately underwhelming, plasticky, cartoony, not unlike the basic animation of South Park. Indeed, when the music does hit a pleasant groove sometimes it feels like a distraction, like the sound of a band wafting in from the next room while a stand-up comedian is in full flow. Generally (although the balance has shifted on recent work like The Eminem Show and the 8 Mile soundtrack), the music is highly subordinate to Eminem's multisyllabic rhyming sprees, dissing and spitting and fighting rap battles on all fronts, seeking out the most morally revolting images with which to send a still puritan, still shockable America scurrying onto its stool, gathering up its skirts.

Eminem has been justly praised for his lyrical invention, his puncturing of US hypocrisy, his scatological, often devastatingly logical wit. He's made an open book of his private life when, at even the most innocuous

EMINEM AND NAS ARE GIVEN AWARDS AT THE DETROIT HIP HOP SUMMIT IN APRIL 2003.

attempt to get past their carefully constructed, heavily glossed self-images, so many celebrities take refuge behind their lawyers and managers. No superstar but him could have written a song like "Stan", for example. No superstar but him would even think to do so. Perhaps that's Eminem's greatest virtue – his raw, untreated honesty.

Yet as much as Eminem praises, he is reviled. He's split public opinion like a melon with a cleaver. There have been those, especially at the beginning of his career, who have resented his whiteness – another classic example of black music being mined and exploited by a paleface opportunist more palatable and non-threatening to the media and industry than the "real" African-American thing. White people buy 70 per cent of hip hop records and there was cynicism in some quarters at the sudden emergence of a "wigger" like Eminem, dream fodder to MTV and *Rolling Stone*. Glibly, he's been dubbed a "black Elvis" and bracketed with that most brazen of insubstantial rap Aryans, Vanilla Ice.

None of which is fair, as Eminem tirelessly retorts. He can point to his career-long association with Dr Dre, who was not in the habit of conferring kudos on white wannabes on the mic. Moreover, unlike the Beastie Boys, who crossed over from punk to rap music, Em has known nothing other than hip hop. He's been steeped almost exclusively in the stuff since his pre-teens. To him, it's natural. Meanwhile, when it comes to his street pedigree, Eminem can claim a distinction. A broken home, an absent father, a violent, dirt-poor childhood, trying to subsist in crack-infested neighbourhoods, even dodging the occasional bullet – Eminem can tick every box. As a poor minority white in the Detroit neighbourhood, he could even claim ethnic minority status, as well as harassment and discrimination from the local ethnic majority.

Eminem's no rap dilettante. He got where he is through verbal combat, besting all-comers in "rap battles" in dingy Detroit hip hop clubs. However, this isn't to say that he's an "honorary African-American", black in every respect except his skin colour. Perhaps that's the reason why, when it comes to using the "N" word he is, unlike, say, Quentin Tarantino, scrupulously politically correct, with one excusable, mixtape aberration unearthed from his teen years, which he was at pains to disavow. His sallow complexion, peroxided hair and, in particular, his non-phat, almost exaggeratedly nerdy rap vocals mark him out as ultra-white.

In some ways, Eminem parallels Jimi Hendrix. Much as Hendrix was one of only a handful of black rockers, so Eminem is one of only a handful of white rappers. And yet much as Hendrix, by virtue of his "blackness" and his consequent experiences, brought something to rock that no white person could, so Eminem arguably brings something to rap, an African-American genre, which no African-American could, or would.

In Eminem's case, it's not just the testimony of the "poor white trash boy". It's a combination of an individualistic determination to pursue his own cultural path regardless of the lack of ethnic company or absence of footsteps to follow, as well as a willingness to belittle, expose and demean himself on record. Perhaps this is part of the penance he subconsciously pays for being the one white guy in an all-black room; what he has to do to get ahead. But in hip hop, assertions of manhood, exaggerated often to the point of obnoxiousness, are a form of over-compensation after decades of racism and discrimination which have, as critic Simon Reynolds once put it, "unmanned" African-Americans. Eminem therefore, as a poor dysfunctional white boy but a white boy nonetheless, has an edge.

Others find Eminem's homophobia and misogyny problematic. They don't buy his constant assertions of freedom of speech. They regard what they see as incitement to hatred of gays and women on his records as an abuse of those freedoms. He's frequently been picketed by the Gay And Lesbian Alliance Against Defamation. He's been roasted for his relentless use of the word "bitch", and for what amount to one-sided attacks (including homicide fantasies) against his mother and his wife Kim, whom he admits have jaundiced his view of womankind in general.

EMINEM AT THE MTV EUROPE AWARDS IN 1999.

There are no easy responses to these questions. Those who idealize Eminem as a satirist of the views he espouses are guilty of wishful thinking; those who regard him as a brave crusader for free speech are foolish. There's no pat justification for Eminem's viler outbursts. However, those who believe Eminem should be gagged or suppressed are equally foolish.

For a start, like any self-respecting obstreperous adolescent, you tell Eminem not to say or do something and he's going to say and do it twice over, because he knows it'll piss you off. He says as much on every record. Secondly, Eminem pours justifiable scorn on the notion that music has the power of suggestion – that kids will go out and murder, rape and shoot people just because his alter ego, Slim Shady, tells them to. Much of what he says on record is a sarcastic demonstration of that point (although much of the time, he's just being bad).

And interestingly, while Eminem has his detractors, he has some unlikely fans. Missy Eliot, who works with victims of domestic abuse, and Elton John, a gay man, are among them. Even Germaine Greer, author of *The Female Eunuch*, one of the seminal texts of modern feminism, admits to being a big Eminem enthusiast. They get it.

So what's to get? Maybe it's this. That Eminem stirs up unease, brings nasty stuff to the surface. American culture is bipartisan in its puritanism. Kids are caught between the Left, which espouses an often stifling and wishful creed of political correctness, and the Right, which proposes a neurotic and anti-permissive creed of censorship and prim morality. Eminem catches a repressed mood of disaffection on the part of kids unable and unwilling to live up to these virtuous ideals. Duly, he flips the finger both ways. Politically he's not a radical or visionary – beneath his delinquent posturing is revealed, again and again, the values of a hardworking, blue-collar conservative, determined to provide for his family by his own honest efforts.

He does, however, realize that the real truth about America doesn't lie in the rigid, bipolar propositions of the finger-waggers but recognizes that the country is slumped somewhere in the middle. He knows it is a dysfunctional mess, and that dysfunctional stories like his, like the unwholesome sagas paraded on daytime "chat shows", are not only the stuff that sells, but basically all that a boy like him has to sell. We're used to reality TV. Eminem is something else – reality music.

Following "Cleaning Out My Closet", however, Eminem seemed to run out of "reality". He'd worked through his immediately family problems, apparently settled all accounts. He had triumphed in every

respect and was more spectacularly successful than he ever dreamed of. All of which brought problems of his own. He no longer had a well of turmoil on which to draw. He was extremely well off, financially utterly secure, under nobody's thumb, no longer doubted by the naysayers, able to do whatever he wanted.

However, successive albums – *Encore*, *Relapse* and *Recovery*, reflected his deep sense of ambivalence to a fame and fortune he'd never sought. You felt an increasing wistfulness for the days when he was struggling, travelling hopefully, back in Detroit, days on which he rapped nostalgic. Yet the murder of his great friend Proof represented a further severance from his past. The mean streets of Detroit had a long reach, but Eminem was too remote to have been able to do anything about his mentor's demise. He felt – nowhere.

Like many in the highest echelons of showbiz, he developed an addiction to painkillers, to combat the feelings of existential futility and loneliness that come from reaching the top and finding there's nothing much there. That became his new drama, his new adversary to wrestle. And, in the third round, with *Recovery*, he won out with a bodyslam.

Eminem is as puerile as ever – his increasing preoccupation with serial killers and the violation of young, emerging female stars like Miley Cyrus, Britney, the Olsen twins and Kim Kardashian, suggests that he sees the threat to his pre-eminence coming from celebrity girl-pop, rather than hip-hop. However, he's shown increasing political maturity, outspoken against George W Bush and the Iraq conflict, tempering some of his initial homophobic discomfort and showing some understanding, especially as his daughters grow up, of being some sort of role model.

Ultimately, Eminem is a difficult, contrary bundle of virtues and vices – asshole, lyrical genius, woman-hater, touchingly sensitive guy, bully, underdog, grossly indecent, thoroughly decent guy. He's inconsistent. He claims his kids are intelligent enough not to be influenced by his records and then he writes "Stan", which proposes precisely the opposite. He does what rock'n'roll, pop and hip hop at their best have always done, and should always do – worry, rather than reassure you, churn you up inside rather than administer blandishments, raise awkward questions rather than dole out pat answers. All this he does and does brilliantly. Which is why he is the biggest star in the world.

11

EMINEM ROCKS THE
HOUSE OF BLUES
IN 1999.

INFINITE

Marshall Bruce Mathers III was initially said to have been born in 1974 or 1975 but when this date was subsequently disputed by his estranged mother, it was conceded that, in fact, he was born on October 17 1972.

He never knew his father, Marshall Bruce Mathers, who was 23 when he married 17-year-old Debbie Scott, the same year their son was born. They had played together in a band called Daddy Warbucks in the two years prior to their marriage, which had taken place against the wishes of Debbie's mother, Betty Kresin. They lived together with Marshall's parents, in the basement of their North Dakota home. However, domestic strains quickly set in and, in circumstances still disputed by Eminem's mother and father decades later, Marshall left Debbie, eventually moving to California. As a teenager, young Marshall attempted to re-establish contact with his father but he was rebuffed, his letters returned unopened. Later, when his son became a millionaire, the elder Marshall would have a mysterious change of heart but Eminem has refused to reconcile with his

father, whose early abandonment of him left him with a primal sense of hurt and rage that would burn through many of his lyrics.

Marshall's early childhood was an unsettled one as he and his mother were forced to shuttle between relatives, between Missouri and Michigan, rarely staying in the same place for six months, as Debbie tried and failed to hold down a series of jobs. It was impossible for the young Marshall to form solid friendships under such circumstances and, inevitably, he became introverted, steeped in comic books and TV. Such an upbringing, while lonely and dysfunctional, has its advantages in the development of a superstar, finding solace in a fantasy world. Marshall Mathers was an outsider too. Accounts from those who knew him at school speak of a quiet, slightly geeky kid who did not make much of a social impact. Even today, in interviews, Eminem can come across as remarkably diffident and soft-spoken.

Eminem's upbringing at the hands of his mother would become a matter of future dispute, litigation and scurrilous lyrics. She insisted that she had brought him up in a stable and loving environment; he portrayed her as a drug addict, a washed-up hippy chick and incompetent parent.

To add to his childhood traumas, when Marshall eventually moved to Detroit, he would suffer a savage beating at the hands of one D'Angelo Bailey, which left him, aged 10, in a coma. He would recount the incident in brutal detail in "Brain Damage" on *The Slim Shady* LP. This wasn't the only time he would be a victim of violence. When his mother moved with him from Warren to Detroit's East Side, he was one of only a handful of white kids in an otherwise all-black neighbourhood, the once thriving "Motor City" of Detroit long since having fallen victim to "white flight" as the post-industrial era set in. En route to school he would have to run the gauntlet of local black kids who would occasionally "jump" him. Yet this didn't generate feelings of racism in Marshall, even after he was stripped of all his clothes at gunpoint by a local black gang. There was very little "white pride" in Marshall.

Indeed, by his early teens he had already become besotted with the nascent hip hop movement, immersing himself in the likes of Run-DMC and LL Cool J, whose eloquent and muscular braggadocio were a fillip to the puny, physically put-upon Marshall. He later got into NWA, tapping into their vicious amoral nihilism, and 3rd Bass, a rap group who, unlike Vanilla Ice, showed that white guys could rap without making corporate dicks of themselves.

He'd been turned onto hip hop by his uncle, Ronnie Pilkington, Debbie's younger brother. They were practically the same age and, although they drifted apart when Ronnie abandoned hip hop for poodle haired rock, Eminem was later devastated to his core when his uncle committed suicide after he was jilted by a girl. It did not help when his mother, in a fit of emotional rage, told her son that she wished he, not Ronnie, had been the one to die. He never forgave her for that remark – it reappears as the sting in the tail of "Cleaning Out My Closet".

When he was 15 years old, Marshall met Proof, a young would-be MC who would later form D12. He started writing his own rap lyrics and even formed his own rap group, Bassmint Productions. All of this came at the expense of his studies. He eventually dropped out of high school having failed ninth grade three times. Although he clearly gave not two damns about school, it nonetheless cut him to the quick when one teacher singled him out in class as someone who would never amount to anything. Another psychological wound, another spur, another angry song in the making (this incident would crop up again on "Revelation", which he cut with D12).

By his own account, Eminem's home life began to suffer in his mid-teens as, time after time, he found himself thrown out of the trailer he shared with his mother. Certainly, as he found work in a variety of menial jobs he would doss down at the houses of various friends, an itinerant once more.

Eminem imersed himself in Detroit's rap scene, coming to the attention of local hip hop producers Marky and Jeff Bass. They've remained with him ever since, although how much they helped "mould" Marshall Mathers is something Eminem's not remarked on much. He performed with groups like the New Jacks and Champtown and, in 1996, released his first single as Soul Intent with the DJ Buttafingas. "Fuckin' Backstabber" (reprised on *Infinite*) was backed with "Biterphobia", which used a loop taken from Andrew Lloyd Webber's *Jesus Christ Superstar* album for its sample.

By this time Marshall was going with Kim Scott, whom he had met when he was 15 and she was 12. A troubled product of a local children's home, Kim was first impressed by Marshall when he performed along to an LL Cool J song atop a coffee table. Initially, they behaved more like fractious siblings but eventually their relationship became sexual, while remaining just as volatile. Still, despite his rap ambitions, there was a certain blue-collar, old-fashioned puritanism about Eminem that prompted him to take his responsibilities as a provider seriously. He took a job as a chef at Gilbert Lodge, where co-workers remember him as generally conscientious. However, he was still dependent in some ways on his mother and still lived in her home

DEBBIE MATHERS-BRIGGS. AFTER FILING A LAWSUIT AGAINST HER SON, SHE BECAME THE TARGET OF HIS MOST SCATHING LYRICS. EX -WIFE KIM (INSET) WAS SIMILARLY ABUSED IN SOME OF EMINEM'S TWISTED TRACKS.

with Kim (who hated Debbie and vice-versa), in an acrid atmosphere of mutual recrimination, emotional strain and resentment. Jennifer Yezvack, a co-worker with Eminem at the grill, was withering in her recollections of Kim's behaviour during this time, accusing her of messing with her husband's head, of blowing hot and cold with him in what was a distinctly on-off relationship. Mind you, Yezvack had an interest to declare as she admitted that she had been Marshall's lover. And it cannot have been an easy time for Kim, but somehow the relationship moved fitfully on, as if under the momentum of the rows and flare-ups between them.

While Kim was pregnant, Marshall recorded his first album, *Infinite*, released on the Bass Brothers' own label, Web Entertainment, after a deal with Jive Records fell through. By now, Eminem had adopted his moniker, a misleadingly cute pun on his own initials and an allusion to the confectionery of the same name. Set to a low-rent, spartan hip hop Bass Brothers and Denaun Porter beat that hardly broke new sound barriers, *Infinite* was an inauspicious debut. Just a thousand vinyl copies were printed up and rather fewer than that sold, although today these original pressings are as sought after as fragments of the true cross. One track, "Searchin'", did receive some

THE BEASTIE BOYS AND RUN-DMC, HIP HOP PIONEERS IDOLIZED BY EMINEM.

limited airplay and one journalist, Marc Kempf, who would later work for Eminem, was early in noticing the rapper's exceptional facility for multisyllabic rhyming. Never subsequently re-released, Eminem has poured retrospective cold water on the album, correctly dismissing it as a derivative effort (Nas and Jay-Z were both conspicuous influences) on which he'd yet to find his own voice or discover his own shadow, the dark self-image which would be his real muse.

At the time, however, Eminem was devastated by the cool reception the album received. It felt like yet another setback in a life which apparently consisted of nothing but setbacks. He thought he'd bombed before he'd begun. In fact, these were the first baby steps of a rap giant in the making. This is Eminem in his innocent phase, unremarkable and as yet untainted by the shit that would make him both miserable and rich.

INFINITE

The title track of the album opens with a crackling verbal salvo, as Em boasts of the "chain reaction" caused by his pen: "To get your brain relaxing, a zany actin' maniac in action…" With frantic scratching of the words "time" and "is money" reflecting the urgency of the deadline an impecunious and desperate Eminem has set himself for superstardom, he attempts to pull out more lyrical stops, bragging that his acappella releases "masterpieces through telekinesis", the sort of elaborate rhyme schemes that so impressed journalist Marc Kempf. However, he's unable to sustain this level of wit and dexterity throughout and often gags on the great chunks of thesaurus he's swallowed, misusing words like "cerebral" and "entity".

IT'S OK

A retrospectively touching lyric this, as a straitened and struggling Eminem puts out thought bubbles for a rosy future, for himself but also his soon-to-be-born baby daughter for whom he hopes to put "half a million" aside. His requests seem almost modest and hardly the aspirations of a wannabe playa in the rap game. He yearns for a happy marriage, old age, everything but the picket fence around the suburban lawn. Prophetically added to his wish list is his very own record label "before my baby can crawl". He's joined by Eye-Kyu on a soothing chorus but gets rather more graphic as he contemplates the "slaughterhouse" or "cesspool" that he considers his life to have been thus far. He yearns for some sort of cleanliness, a "better life for my daughter and spouse". He describes his manful efforts to grapple with life's vicissitudes, to keep his spirits up, do the right thing, and avoid doing "shit illegal". The image of his half-brother Nathan, dodging the crack addicts as he puts in the school hours could be part of some hip hop update of Stevie Wonder's ghetto classic "Living For The City".

Eminem wouldn't make his millions by talking up these essentially decent and sanguine hardworking values to America's youth, and this side of him, though just as "real" as any other, wasn't one we'd see much more of, especially as disillusionment blackened his soul. He even invokes God here, but this piety would eventually disappear from the Eminem lyrical landscape altogether. However, this lyric does show his willingness to tell truths about himself, to put heartfelt statements on wax, rather than sublimate every last ounce of his efforts into cartoon blowhardery. It reflects his vulnerability – but also a will of iron.

313

Taking its title from the Detroit area phone code, here Eminem reverts to the verbose cockiness of the aspiring rap jouster, again dropping multisyllabic cluster bombs with an occasional disregard for meaning or reason ("everything that you collaborate I lacerate"). In the chorus, he bigs himself up as a "sweet MC", a faintly jarring effeminacy. But he roams across the rest of the verses like a blustery rap superman, shoving dynamite up the asses of his MC rivals, deriding their efforts on the mic and reverentially namechecking his early hero, LL Cool J, a hip hop paradigm in his own mind. Still, "313" is a little long on bombast, a little short on wit.

TONIGHT

Against a female chorus chanting the title, Eminem's fevered wordplay becomes almost James Joycean here, as his syllables bleed into one another, both losing and somehow multiplying their meaning ("Druggling thugs, smuggling drugs… gaffling tracks"). This is goodtime hands-in-the-air stuff, bearing none of the ill-will that was as essential to his later material as oil to a car engine. "We don't want no one feeling uptight", runs the chorus.

Eminem even puts out a saucy call to the "finest women in the audience". In subsequent live shows he would adopt this sort of flirtatious charm with the ladies, but lyrically it's rare for Em to refer to the opposite sex in such polite terms. Strange that, although Eminem was dirt-poor when he wrote these rhymes, he exhibits a joie de vivre here that's nonexistent in his multi-millionaire phase.

MAXINE

A duet with fellow D12-er Kon Artis, this kicks off with a spot of telephone dialogue in which the strung-out anti-heroine of the title idly toys with Artis, before Eminem delivers the low-down on this disreputable female, an HIV positive crack addict, a foul and unclean temptress whom any self-respecting man should avoid unless they wish to place themselves in "jeopardation".

We're left in no doubt about Maxine's depravity (her behaviour in a second phone call certainly doesn't help the case for the defence) as she ensnares Kon Artis before revealing she has AIDS. However, although Maxine presents an easy and obvious target, both Eminem and Kon Artis refrain from any imaginative exclamations of homicidal misogyny such as Slim Shady might have indulged in. Rather, this is a more graphic hip hop version of Cliff Richard's "Devil Woman".

NWA – NIGGAZ WITH ATTITUDE – THE LEGENDARY, INFAMOUS INNOVATORS OF GANSTA RAP WHO LAUNCHED EMINEM'S PRODUCER DR DRE TO FAME.

OPEN MIC

Joined by fellow local rapper Thyme, Eminem relives here the world of rap battles at Detroit's Hip Hop Shop, those merciless duels at the mic, hip hop's own bread and circuses recreated in *8 Mile*, in which the baying of the audience would determine which of the combatants would be thrown to the lions of derision. Although Em doesn't discuss the anxieties he had when he first went up to the mic, particularly on account of his skin colour, Thyme's scratched-up chorus does recreate the sort of intimidating catcalls that would have rung through Eminem's head in those early days ("Who the fuck passed you the mic and said that you can flow?").

Again, Em's juvenile exuberance and ambition over-reach his skills a little here, although occasionally the verbosity pays off ("Slicing up an enemy's appendages till he haemorrhages"), and there is an early, witty flash of scatological eloquence ("You couldn't flip shit playing in toilets with a spatula").

NEVER 2 FAR

On this track, Eminem revisits the hard times schtick of "It's OK", although there's an edge of nervous desperation here rather than daydreaming. It commences with a spot of dialogue between Eminem and a buddy on a street corner, rummaging around for spare cents for the bus fare, before the humiliation of it all bursts over Eminem like a sudden shower and he loses it, ranting at the despair of being 21 (he was, even more demeaningly, actually 23) and still living with his mother.

As ever, Eminem marks himself out as a creature of the American Dream, in which individual achievement, rather than social improvement, provides the solution. The philosophical upshot of this is pretty trite, as outlined in the chorus: "You can do anything… 'cause you can be a star/No matter wherever you are…". Em is revealing his ambivalence towards money. On "It's OK" it was the "root of all evil". Now, money is the only route out of town.

Eminem would never really depart from this philosophy, as "Lose Yourself" would show. Nor would he abandon the posse he namechecks and pledges faith to here, the "crews true and divine" who all appear on *Infinite*. The principles espoused on "Never 2 Far" may be banal, but at least Eminem lived up to them to the maximum.

SEARCHIN'

EMINEM'S HOUSE
IN 2001 WAS
AN ENORMOUS
CHANGE FROM THE
SURROUNDINGS HE
GREW UP IN.

The one track from *Infinite* that received any airplay, and perhaps the reason why Eminem has never been anxious for this album to resurface, "Searching" is an utterly besotted love letter from Eminem to Kim, the recollection of which would make his cheeks burn with shame and even resentment at having committed such an embarrassing piece of doggerel to wax. All that's missing here are love-hearts in the margins as Em rattles off the platitudes, reliving the "snuggling and teasing", the "kissing and hugging and squeezing".

It gets worse as Eminem goes all moonstruck when he thinks of the way Kim's lips "sparkle and glare in the sun", and then lays himself completely open, soft and squishy, wondering if he may "be your man legally wed".

In the chorus, Eminem talks about how Kim is "the only one I want in my life, baby". Strangely, this turns out to have been true, thus far. His relationship with Kim has been the only significant and long-term one in his life, even during its prolonged and eventually terminal "off" phase. That he felt so ardently for her that he was prepared to compromise his dignity with these valentine card verses accounts for how hard he would take Kim's rejection of him. Hell hath no fury like an Eminem scorned.

BACKSTABBER

The first ever Eminem single (recorded on the proceeds of a tax refund) is reprised here. In its vindictiveness and graphic vengeance, it offers a limited glimpse of Eminem's as-yet undeveloped dark side. There's a comical touch as an APB is radioed out to police, who are instructed to look out for a suspect with green hair armed with a knife, with which he's liable to stab you in the back. The rap takes the form of a lurid comic book-style fantasy, with the police setting up roadblocks and keeping full radio contact as they seek out the miscreant, with a warning going out that "he might be one of our own guys". Finally, Eminem himself wreaks violence on the oily, two-timing, insincere asshole, jabbing him in the spleen with a knife and beating his head with a telephone.

And yet, for all its lurid adventures, "Backstabber" is moral at heart, a hip hop update (though not cover) of the O' Jays song of the same name. Here, a righteous Eminem helps hunt down a malevolent gremlin who represents "vice" – in this case, the vice of deceitfulness, always an anathema to the overly candid Mr Mathers. In future recordings, it would be Eminem, aka Slim Shady, who played the bad guy, the sleazebag on the run. And never again would he extend to the police the sort of good-citizenly cooperation that he demonstrates on "Backstabber".

JEALOUSY WOES II

Another paean to Kim, this, although this time, over a taunting, chanting chorus, it's distinctly less rosy, highlighting the strife that had continually riven their relationship. Here, coming home after a hard double shift in which he's stopped off only to buy his girlfriend a gift, Eminem's greeted by a tetchy girlfriend, almost at once busting his balls, dissing, interrogating him, convinced he's been seeing some other girl. He tries to pacify her, wishes they didn't have to quarrel, but then acidly observes that she's turned into a "gangsta bitch". He also puts it to her that she's been telling friends that she plans to dump Em and here his temperature rises ominously. His fists clench as he talks of "wanting to smack her face in".

Eminem doesn't go so far as to name Kim personally, and camouflages the song with some dialogue superimposed over the chorus in which the use of the otherwise taboo word "nigga" is an indicator that neither Em nor Kim are involved in this particular scenario. Em never uses the word in any of his material – even as it's deployed in verse three it's via a sample – but this song, in which Eminem further accuses his girlfriend of "acting like my ex-wife" is prophetic of the storm clouds that were about to break over his and Kim's relationship.

THE SLIM SHADY EP

Not only did Eminem have to cope with *Infinite* having gone down like a very small, lead balloon in the hip hop world, but he also had to deal with the responsibilities of fatherhood, as his beloved Hailie Jade was born on Christmas Day 1996. He would always shower unbridled love and affection on Hailie, determined to provide her with the sort of parenting he felt he'd been deprived of himself. However, her arrival spelt a period of domestic misery as he struggled to keep up rental payments, even as he worked up to 60 hours a week at Gilbert's Lodge. He was forced to move his family from hovel to hovel, much as his own mother had in his childhood years. The only place they could afford to live was in a crack-addled district of Detroit, along 7 Mile, in which they were subjected to repeated burglaries, a whispering campaign of racial harassment and even a stray bullet which lodged in the wall of the kitchen while Kim was washing up.

It was during this period that Kim briefly left Eminem, taking Hailie with her. According to Eminem, Kim had developed a contempt for his inability to provide for the family. Em knew it was true. "It was like, fuck, I can't afford to buy my daughter diapers," he told *Rolling Stone*. Yet, even though they reunited shortly afterwards, moving back in with Eminem's mother, he never forgot or forgave this act of betrayal, which would inspire the hideous anti-shrine he conceived for her in the form of "'97 Bonnie & Clyde".

Eminem's salvation would come in the form of the Slim Shady character. He told The Source that the notion of Slim came to him as he was taking a dump. It immediately triggered off a series of rhymes and associations and, pretty soon, Shady began to ooze black onto the scribbling pad, as Em began to excrete a fully formed persona, the dark, malodorous, anti-social side of his character which he intended to smear across pop culture like a dirty protest – a more psychotic version of South Park's hid-e-ho-ing Mr Hanky, The Christmas Poo, maybe.

According to the Bass Brothers, though, they had played a part in encouraging Eminem to explore his nastier side. "We came up with the idea

of shock rap," they claimed. They may indeed have discussed with Eminem the idea of digging deeper into the nasty stuff inside him. After all, they had lost money on *Infinite* and would have been anxious to analyze what had gone wrong in the hope of making good on their investment. However, their claim that "shock rap" was an entirely novel creation was untrue – there were precedents in the likes of NWA and the Geto Boys, even the sleazy, moronic 2 Live Crew.

All the same, Slim Shady would bring some poison to the party that no one had ingested before. Although initially received in some quarters as a cynical attempt on the part of a cocky Caucasian to carjack the rapsploitation genre, the creation of Slim Shady can be seen in retrospect as one last,

desperate heave from a man who, during this period, had already attempted suicide (see "Rock Bottom"). All he had left to throw up were the dregs of his soul, his toxic bile. Everything was at stake. He simply had to succeed. As Eminem was to later observe, "If I didn't, then my producers were going to give up on the whole rap thing we were doing. [so] I made some shit that I wanted to hear."

And so, having jettisoned the game but too-nice guy of *Infinite*, Eminem embarked on The *Slim Shady EP*, an eight-track collection recorded in about two weeks in late 1997, which represented a leap on from his debut album, in terms of style, confidence and musical chops. Even his D12 crew had been a little shocked when he delivered an early impromptu showcase of his new persona. Bizarre, who would casually go on to rap about slitting his grandmother's throat, declared that this was the work of "a white boy on drugs". Proof suggested he'd headed way too far over the top with this new "drugs shit". But that was kind of the point. He'd been under the bottom for too long.

LOW, DOWN, DIRTY

Eminem introduces the reptilian Slim Shady to the world by slapping an "R" restricted on himself and claiming to have shot himself in the neck. Declaring himself to have split into two separate Jekyll and Hyde-style personae, he comes on like the little boy in *The Shining*, possessed by psychotic voices: "Murder, murder, redrum". He's insane, he's cracked like the mirror he stands in front of on the front cover of the EP, he's lost it – "hid in the bush

like Margot Kidder" (a reference to the actress who played Lois Lane in the Superman movies but who went completely off the rails, and was indeed found in 1996 in a garden in Glendale, California, hiding behind a bush, dishevelled and babbling incoherently).

The pop cultural references now come thick and fast, with Bette Midler getting a namecheck, and Eminem gibbering multisyllabically and maniacally. He takes time out to stand back in amazement at himself, even cheeks his old friend Proof by quoting back at him his own criticism about the "drugs shit" he was indulging in here.

IF I HAD…

After the ostentatious insanity and fantasy rampaging of "Low, Down, Dirty", " If I Had…" sees Eminem take a long, straight, hard look at his life in a mirthless, deadpan monotone that allows for no illusions or consolations. It was written one cold winter's day when, on top of all the other miseries life was heaping on him, his car had broken down. Against a tolling, deathly riff, Eminem addresses us like a nihilist who's commandeered the pulpit. What is life? What are friends? What is money? He asks rhetorically, providing his own bleak responses.

Friends are "really your enemies", he concludes bitterly – Eminem was wary of other people even before fame made him prey, as he saw it, to two-faced leeches who only wanted a piece of him. Money is the "root of all evil" he says distrustfully, repeating the sentiments of "It's OK" on *Infinite*. Life is an obstacle which brings you to the ground. "I'm tired of life," he declares, in a voice that sounds drained of all emotion.

Then the song really takes off as Eminem delivers a breakdown of all the reasons he's tired of life, each handpicked from his recent experiences. He's tired of finding refuge in Hennessy, tired of the crack addicts and hoodlums in his neighbourhood who make his domestic life unbearable, "spraying shit and dartin' off", tired of having no money, a minimum wage job, of being "white trash, broke and dirt poor", of DJs not playing his record but "your shit" instead.

Line by line, he paints an authentic and deeply felt picture of a life of poverty, degradation, frustration and loserdom that is absolutely the antithesis of hip hop's usual retreat into gangsta or pimp fantasy. The whole world seems to be against him. Small wonder then, that even if the million bucks he craves were to come his way, it wouldn't restore his already-

AN EARLY PUBLICITY
SHOT IN NEW YORK
CITY 1998.

25

broken goodwill. Instead, he indulges in misanthropic fantasies, promising that, if he makes it, he'll use his wherewithal to "make the world suck my dick", or buy a brewery to "turn the whole world into alcoholics". Even at this very early stage, he's garnering a trickle of adverse feedback from the media, to which he angrily responds: "How'm I supposed to be positive when I don't see shit positive?"

Finally, this slow-moving cyclone of woe winds down as Eminem reveals his real beef – that he can't get any airplay. And, all spent, he concludes with a rueful gesture, an "It's OK". Not unlike Samuel Beckett's "I Can't Go On, I'll Go On", really.

"If I Had…" was one of three tracks featured on *The Slim Shady LP*, with Dina Rae's soulful backing vocals sanctifying Eminem's unholy, bitter rap fermentation.

JUST DON'T GIVE A FUCK

Eminem wrote this coming out of an off-the-rails period of drug-taking and boozing, as his domestic responsibilities mounted up and threatened to overwhelm him, and, crucially, as the Bass Brothers threatened to pull the plug on his rap career.

This is effectively the Eminem manifesto Mark II, containing as it does the very first rhymes Em scribbled down when he conceived the character. "Slim Shady, brain dead like Jim Brady", a sick allusion to the White House press secretary who had taken a bullet to the head meant for President Reagan back in 1981 and had suffered paralysis and speech impairment ever since.

This feels more like it should have been the opening salvo to the EP but here it is, better late than never, with Eminem joined by rapper Frogg, who urges everyone to "wave their hands in the air" before affecting to think better of it, as this isn't the usual rap fare.

Over a frantic backbeat, parping, wheezing and levering zanily like some hip hop Heath Robinson contraption, Eminem delivers the chorus like a hooligan hurling a pint of lager across a bar room. "I JUST DON'T GIVE A FUUUCCCKK!"

AT AN MTV AWARDS CEREMONY, WILL SMITH REMARKED THAT HE DIDN'T NEED TO RESORT TO BAD LANGUAGE TO SELL HIS RECORDS. EMINEM FELT HE'D BEEN DISSED.

"I think maybe my attitude attracts a lot of kids, especially white kids from the suburbs and stuff," he told the NME in an interview following his first tour of the UK. "They wanna have this attitude like they don't give a fuck. They love their Tupacs and their Biggies and the whole image, and when someone comes along and goes against the grain and just truly doesn't give a fuck, they wanna be that person. Cos I know when I was younger and the Beastie Boys came out, they seemed like they didn't give a fuck, and when NWA came out, they really didn't give a fuck. The whole attitude attracts people."

With Eminem, there's more to the message than merely showing the finger. Do your worst, he's saying, the worst has already done to me. And now he's become the worst, transmogrified into Slim Shady, diseased, lethal, pistol-packing and profane. "The looniest, zaniest, spontaneous sporadic impulsive thinker", he spits, raiding the dictionary like a skinny, white Don King, "Compulsive drinker, addict, half animal, half man".

By verse three, we see Slim recall his "old" self as puny Eminem, head down and quiet as a mouse in school. In real life, the young Marshall Mathers pumped iron in the hope of staving off the sort of bullies liable to kick sand

at him. In this song, he undergoes a Marvel comic book-style transformation after drinking whiskey in the eighth grade and runs amok, "raping the women's swim team". (This line was cut from the version of the song that appears on *The Slim Shady LP*). "Don't take me for a joke," he warns, as he was wont to when he'd just perpetrated a ludicrous or outrageous line – as if to let us know that the events depicted here may be false, but the bad feelings that give rise to their creation are very real.

Here was the duality of Eminem in full. The "real" Eminem probably gave too

EMINEM WAS ABOUT TO BECOME ONE OF THE MOST INFAMOUS FIGURES IN THE HISTORY OF RAP.

much of a fuck, then and now, about everything. His mom, Kim, his friends, his enemies, his career, his daughter – whether loving or hating, he tended towards over-sensitivity, taking things too much to heart. However, as Slim Shady he could experience and share with his fans the catharsis of casting off all his concerns and woes, his shyness and his frustrations, cocking a leg at the world and letting rip a big one.

JUST THE TWO OF US

This was the first appearance of the song that would be renamed "'97 Bonnie & Clyde" when it appeared on *The Slim Shady LP*, a song destined, when it received wider exposure, to become one of Eminem's most infamous.

With DJ Head twisting the melodic line of the original Bill Withers song (once featured in a British Heineken advert featuring a castaway and a crab), this song is unnervingly profanity-free, addressed as it is to Hailie, brimful of the love Eminem has for his little daughter. "Just The Two Of Us" would be one of the most gloopily sentimental pieces of mush and babytalk ever laid down on tape. (Indeed, it mimics Will Smith's own, oppressively soft-centred hip hop take on the Withers original). However, it soon dawns on the listener that it isn't just the two of them. Hai-Hai's mother is in the trunk of the car and they're driving out to the beach in order to dispose of the body.

Eminem tells Hailie the smell of the corpse is actually coming from a skunk, covers up for the trip by saying that mom is "taking a little nap" in the trunk and that she fancies a late night swim. He explains away the wound on her slit throat as a scratch, the blood she's covered in as ketchup. "Mommy's too sweepy to hear you," he burbles babyishly.

Eminem's explained to Hailie about heaven, hell and prison and that Da-Da is going to "all of them, except one". Finally, he has Hailie help him tie a rope around her mom's leg as he attaches a rock to it, in order to heave the body over the harbour side. Perturbingly, Eminem drops in the "'97 Bonnie & Clyde" reference, with all its connotations of a deeply unhealthy alliance, implicating the innocent infant as accessory to the crime. This is exacerbated by Em's use of Hailie, gurgling away in the background in her first studio appearance. And it isn't just mom that's in the trunk, but we are to infer, the new man Kim has shacked up with, whom Eminem has also murdered.

This fantasy scenario had been churning around Eminem's imagination during the summer of 1997, when he and Kim were temporarily estranged, with Kim indeed threatening to take out a restraining order. Em's strongest emotion was the fear of losing Hailie rather than missing Kim and "Just The Two Of Us", despite its deeply controversial subject matter, is essentially an (admittedly perverse) love song to his daughter. As Eminem himself said, his first thought was "How can I make a song about Hailie?" Not wishing to "make the shit corny or nothing", he decided to introduce a corrective dose of homicidal frenzy.

"Just The Two Of Us" in itself doesn't mark Eminem out as a psychopath. Part of its brilliance and authenticity is that it captures perfectly the sort of seething mindset that most of us fall prey to now and again. "Just The Two Of Us" is precisely the sort of vengeful fantasy many people are apt to play out mentally when they feel scorned or crossed – even if, like Eminem, they don't act them out for real.

What is appalling, thrilling, grossly unfair and brilliantly audacious is that Eminem should have put out such a fantasy on record – and kept it on, even after he and Kim had made up. For Eminem its use was justified as it was a great "concept song" with universal applications, the more so for being forged in the heat of an emotional extreme.

As with "Kim", he explained that the song was proof of the – ahem – warm feelings he had for her. She didn't really buy it, however, and who can blame her? "When I played her the song she bugged the fuck out," Eminem told *Rolling Stone*, especially as he had told her he was taking Hailie to Chuck E Cheese when he was taking her to the studio.

Moreover, Eminem had never anticipated that the song would reach any sort of audience beyond Detroit. There was no deal in the offing with Interscope. Perhaps he was rather disingenuous when he professed surprise at the stink the song caused, not just with his wife but with the public. Or it could be that he (as well as his production team, The Bass Brothers, and Interscope) realized that, as Jerry Springer discovered, there's gold in that thar trash; that real-life dysfunction and the airing of lowlife laundry sells big in the US. If you've got it, sell it. Whatever, like the audiences at Mel Brooks' "Springtime For Hitler" in his film *The Producers*, we're aghast but transfixed.

There was a postscript to "'97 Bonnie & Clyde" when Tori Amos did an implicitly reproachful cover version of it on her album *Strange Little Girls*. A victim of domestic abuse herself, she defended Em's right to put the song out because the "male rage in it is real", and there was nothing to be gained in repressing such thoughts. However, while acknowledging the "empathy" created by Eminem's impassioned delivery of the song, which, she admitted, even she felt, she wanted her version to provide a conduit for Kim, who was silent on the original. "She has to have a voice," said Amos.

NO ONE'S ILLER THAN ME

Following on from "Just The Two Of Us", it's hard to disagree with the proposal of the title, although in fact this is a friendly rap battle for the honour between Eminem, fellow D12 posse members Swifty and Bizarre, and rapper Fuzz. Swifty talks of making "quadriplegics" out of "non-rappin' rejects" the ever-entertainingly vile Bizarre offhandedly relates how he was recently administered a blow job by a transvestite, murdered his grandmother (not the last time the poor lady was to fall victim to Bizarre's peculiar grandmatricidal instincts) and had an affair with his 10-year-old niece. You sometimes get the feeling with Bizarre that he's being just the teeniest little bit facetious.

Eminem joins in the general tone of things the way he swills and spits his syllables is something else: "Stab your abdomen with a handcrafted pocketknife and spill your antacid" isn't a daft incitement to violence, it's a brilliant flight of phonetic fancy and would have been taken as such by its intended audience, if not its unintended one.

MURDER, MURDER

A remixed version of this track appeared on the *Next Friday* soundtrack. Kicking off with a steal from Tupac Shakur's "Outlaw" ("All I see is murder, murder, my mind state"), it's a fantasy Slim Shady heist, in which Eminem once and for all forfeits his soul in the pursuit of millions ("See I'm a nice man but money turned me into Satan"). It's a maliciously detailed account of a bank robbery in which Slim has left at least one man and two women dead, the sort of "pain in the ass innocent bystanders" who so irritated Clemenza in *The Godfather.* Significantly, even in this X-rated comic strip nasty, there's a vestige of truth and tenderness – he's doing it all for his daughter Hailie ("I got a daughter to feed"). Finally, he gives himself up to the cops but, anticipating the logic of his future would-be censors, he pleads diminished responsibility. It wasn't him that did it but the "gangsta rap" and the booze. Sue them.

31

THE SLIM SHADY LP

Eminem's precipitate rise to fame and notoriety began in January 1998, when he signed to Dr Dre's label Aftermath. According to fellow D-12 member Bizarre, Eminem had gone missing for three weeks, only to return aglow with what must have sounded like a tall tale about having hung out with Dre at his condo.

Em first came to Dre's attention when a tape of *The Slim Shady EP* was played to him at the house of Jimmy Iovine, CEO of Interscope, parent label to Aftermath. Interscope's reps had picked up the tape out at the LA Rap Olympics. There, Eminem was placed second following six vicious rounds of verbal smackdowns, but he was denied a spot in the final in what some considered the worst, most dubious decision since Roy Jones Jr was denied a boxing gold medal at the 1988 Seoul Olympics. "He was so far ahead of the rest of the competition it was embarrassing," said Dean Geistlinger of Interscope. Miserable and aggrieved, Em barely acknowledged Geistlinger when he requested a tape of the EP. Yet this exchange, the memory of which quickly dissolved in Eminem's distraught mood, would prove a catalyst for an introduction to the NWA producer whom he'd idolized since his early teens.

Born Andre Young in South Central Los Angeles in 1965, Dr Dre was a musical child prodigy and inevitably became involved in the fledgling hip hop scene at an early age. He started musical life with the World Class Wreckin' Cru, but the make-up and sequins they donned onstage marked them out as relics of rap's showbizzy Triassic era at a time when the likes of Run-DMC were cutting a toughened-up and dressed-down mode of hip hop.

Dre then became involved with Eazy E (Eric Wright) who had formed his own label, Ruthless Records, allegedly with the proceeds of drugs money. Eazy put up bail for Dre following a misdemeanour, asking in return that he produce records for Ruthless. From this agreement evolved NWA (Niggas With Attitude), whose 1989 debut *Straight Outta Compton* effectively marked the birth of gangsta rap. With cuts like "Gangsta Gangsta" and "Fuck Tha Police", NWA were the most frightening and amoral reflection of ghetto life yet committed to vinyl. There was no Curtis Mayfield-style lamentation here, no Public Enemy-style call to arms. "Do I look like a motherfuckin' role model?" asked Ice Cube. Rather, this was street life in the raw, uncensored and, it seemed to many, celebrating a lifestyle in which pump-action shotguns, drugs, illicitly earned dollars and ugly misogyny featured prominently.

Attacked from both left and right for their political content, ostracized by the media and even the subject of an FBI dossier, NWA nonetheless sold three million copies of their debut album. Indeed, the moral panic they whipped up served only to bolster both their outlaw status and their sales figures (a lesson the would-be censors and moral guardians have never learned).

However, just two years later, NWA fell victim to internal strife and the predatory attentions of Suge Knight, fearsome head of Death Row records, who, understanding that NWA's success owed as much to Dre's phat, low-riding, funky backbeats as to its lyrical content, lured the Doctor away. In time, however, disenchanted by the hideous culture of violence engendered by Death Row, which culminated in the East Coast/West Coast rap wars and the deaths of both the Notorious B.I.G and Tupac Shakur, Dre quit the label and set up his own label, Aftermath.

FELLOW RAPPER DR DRE KICK-STARTED EMINEM'S CAREER

Although he'd been running the label for some months, Dre would later say that never had he come across fresh talent via a demo tape. Immediately

knocked sideways by the sheer energy, invention and insolence of Eminem's rhymes, though, Dre decided he needed to call this guy. He claimed he had no idea that Eminem was white, although Em's reedy, Caucasian intonations must have offered a clue. The way Dre tells the story – "find that kid and sign him up!" – belies an element of calculation also. Interscope, parent label to Aftermath, would have been aware of the potential, as well as the potential pitfalls, of attempting to foist a white "shock rapper" on the world, and would have spent a while weighing up the pros and cons. Eventually, however, a few months after the Rap Olympics, a call was put through to the Bass Brothers, whose number was on the cassette. Finally, news reached Marshall Mathers that Dr Dre wanted to meet him.

Eminem flipped. "Don't lie to me. Don't fuckin' lie to me!" he screamed over and over, when he got the news from the Bass Brothers. Just months earlier he'd been ODing on pills, his wife had left him, his rap career looked to have about as much of a future as Detroit's car industry. Now, who knows how, he was up for an audience with Dr Dre. It took a while to bring him down from the ceiling, but once he'd calmed down he made the flight to LA to meet Dre.

Considerately, Dre didn't prolong the agonising wait in the Aftermath offices and once he'd introduced himself to Eminem, the relationship sparked off immediately. His initial nerves abated, Eminem loosened up and, over the next seven days, a series a highly creative studio sessions yielded a number of fresh tracks, as Eminem freestyled off Dre's bouncing backbeats. "As soon as we got into the studio we knocked off four songs in six hours," said Eminem. "Every beat he would make, I had a rhyme for." These would provide the foundations for *The Slim Shady LP*, Eminem's second album proper.

Dr Dre's endorsement conferred instantaneous credibility on Eminem. He was by no means the first white rapper but he was certainly the first to arrive

D12'S SWIFT AND KON ARTIS.

on the scene with this sort of letter of introduction. Later, Eminem said that Dre's offer was not the only one on the table at that time, but no option could compete with the chance not only to be signed by but to work with Dre. Word spread of Dre's peroxide protegé, in the several months running up to the February 1999 release of *The Slim Shady LP.* There was a national tour, as well as the release of "Just Don't Give A Fuck", Em's masterly exercise in boorish defiance, coupled with "Brain Damage", which was a top ten US single. But it was with "My Name Is" that America got its first spiked dollop of Eminem (even with toned down lyrics), with an accompanying video featuring Em mimicking everyone from President Clinton to Marilyn Manson, a select pantheon of '90s controversy generators which he himself was on the point of joining.

When the album was finally released, it sold half a million copies in its first fortnight, entering the Billboard charts at no. 2. By the end of the year, it had already sold three million copies. He made the cover of *Rolling Stone* in April, sporting tattoos reading "Kim" and "Rot In Pieces" on his abdomen (The couple had been reconciled, Kim having apparently having revised her previous assessment of Eminem as a poor provider). The likes of Spin went

FUNKMASTER
FLEX, DR DRE AND
EMINEM AT THE 2000
AMERICAN MUSIC
AWARDS.

35

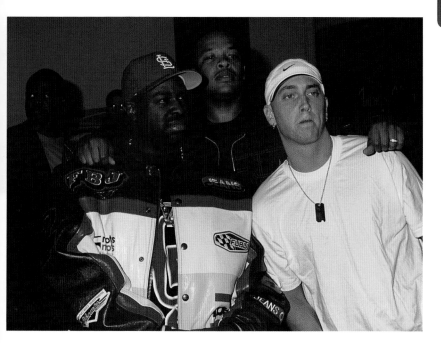

into raptures over this "white trash Don Rickles" and the *LA Times* honoured him with a full-length feature. Some complained that Eminem's success was yet another example of a white co-opting black music and that he was enjoying the sort of sales denied to more deserving African-American rappers. Others, however, shrewdly observed that Eminem's success was down to his willingness to 'fess up to his personal inadequacies and humiliatingly impoverished upbringing, an exhilarating change from the usual, numbingly unconvincing spiels about champagne and gold chains to which much of hip hop was still prone.

For all those who lauded Eminem's appalling yet undeniably entertaining outpourings of unbridled, uncensored freestyling, obscenely hilarious and venomous; his multi-headed persona, his slaloming turns of phrase on tracks like "Role Model" and "Bad Meets Evil", others were simply disgusted. *Billboard*'s editor Timothy White argued over the course of a full-page editorial that Eminem was "exploiting the world's misery", while America's Victim Support Group castigated him for "making money out of horrific crimes". Most disturbing was "'97 Bonnie & Clyde", formerly "Just The Two Of Us", on which Eminem acted out a scenario, depicted in grainy black and white on the album cover, in which he murdered his wife and then packed her into the trunk Goodfellas-style, all the while explaining to his little daughter that they were just taking mommy for a swim, as he dumps her body into the water.

Many critics at this stage were not quite clear that this wasn't just misogynistic fantasy – one compared it to something you might expect from Garth Brooks. They were unaware of just how close to home this lyric was, that the gurgling little girl was Eminem's own daughter, too young yet to discover the role she had played in this hideously compelling fantasy about the death of her own mother.

In Britain, Eminem had a tougher time making headway. He was initially treated with scepticism, even disdain, particularly when he played a show at London's Ladbroke Grove Subterrania which ended after just five numbers, with angry punters demanding their money back. A Channel 4 documentary later showed the rapper urinating against a wall in Soho, shouting abuse at passers by. "Potential superstar or one hit wonder arsehole?" wondered the NME.

The album sleeve image of Eminem, his t-shirt bloodied as he stares out goofily from a cartoon backdrop, certainly suggested the possibility that he was a sharp interloper making a quick but huge killing on a single tidal wave of hooh-hah, a wacky Caucasian anomaly, Vanilla with attitude, a hip hop Itchy And Scratchy.

Speaking to NME, Eminem played up these cartoon credentials. "I don't take life as seriously as a lot of people," he said. "I take responsibility for what I say but not everything is to be taken so literal. My shit is not politically correct. I look at it like a South Park episode. It's obvious. Unless you're really insane." However, for Eminem, life was about to get very serious indeed – and the insanity was about to begin for real.

PUBLIC SERVICE ANNOUNCEMENT

Performed by Jeff Bass of FBT productions, "Public Service Announcement" is an ass-covering caveat for the contents of the album that is to follow, while at the same time it mocks the earnest culture of advisory stickers and didactic admonitions to wayward teens. "The views and events expressed here are totally fucked," warns Bass. However, he also warns that the album is "not to be taken lightly" and advises that children's laces should be removed from their shoes, in the manner of prisoners on suicide watch, before they be exposed to its contents. Finally, as a patently tacked on afterthought, Eminem takes the mic and, with deadpan sarcasm tells America's kids, "Don't do drugs."

EMINEM QUICKLY ESTABLISHED A DEVOTED FANBASE.

37

MY NAME IS

One of the earliest tracks Eminem and Dre worked on together in their initial, whirlwind sessions, and the track which Em would have a hard time both living up to and living down, "My Name Is" is a classic piece of strychnine-laced alcopop, with Eminem coming on like the hired clown at a birthday party who turns the little kids onto porn and video nasties while the parents are in the kitchen. The scrunched, loping chorus line sees Em's head pop out from all manner of unexpected holes, like one of those mischievous weasels you try and hit with a rubber mallet at the fairground.

The opening lines see Em get the "attention of the class" in Slim Shady mode, egging the kids on to see him "stick nine inch nails through one of my eyelids" and to emulate his fantasy life of drugs, violence and general, fucked up desperation. Again, the joke is on the censors and their risible "monkey see, monkey do" ethos when it comes to protecting children.

Then, a complete non-sequitur as he wonders which Spice Girl to impregnate, before, without missing a beat, he slips into autobiographical mode ("Ever since I was 12 I've felt like I'm someone else"), his poor academic career ("next semester I'll be 35") and his mother's shortcomings ("I just

found out she did more dope than I do!"). Alone, this would have amounted to a luckless, self-deprecating account but it's studded with vituperative blasts of pure fantasy about "ripping Pamela Lee's tits off" or vengefully stapling his English teacher's nuts to a stack of papers, as Dr Dre looks on, mock-aghast: "Slim Shady, you a basehead!"

After further malicious, tangential nonsense involving pedestrians and spaceships, Em winds up on a (sort of) Oedipal note, whining at his mom for her breastfeeding inadequacies ("You ain't got no tits!") before mirthlessly recounting a dream in which he slit his father's throat. Eminem's father was of the absentee variety, making a reappearance when his son became famous but receiving the cold shoulder he'd given Eminem when the latter had written to him in his teens.

With its silly sound FX, "My Name Is" implicitly mocks the sullen, heavy-duty ambience of much gangsta rap and helps stress that Slim Shady is more of a fictional Lord of Misrule than a Menace II Society. Cultural commentator Nelson George pointed out that, despite the outrageous content of his songs, Eminem's whiteness ultimately made him less threatening to American mainstream audiences. "God sent me to piss the world off!" cries Eminem joyfully on "My Name Is". Piss the world off indeed, but not scare the living crap out it.

That said, Labi Siffre, whose "I Got The" was sampled on "My Name Is", successfully objected to its unsavoury lyrics, particularly a bit about raping lesbians, which meant that it had to be heavily toned down for mass market consumption.

Brilliantly infectious, "My Name Is" is more than mere lampoonery. Unbeknownst to his freshly acquired mass audience, Eminem was touching on some raw home truths, the full extent of which would become clear when his mother, on the strength of the aspersions first cast on her here, eventually filed a $10 million lawsuit against her son.

EMINEM IN 1999,
KEEPING IT WEIRD.

GUILTY
CONSCIENCE

Another Dre/Eminem collaboration laid down in the course of a week, "Guilty Conscience" is among Em's funniest pieces, casting him as it does in the role of scary, trigger-happy white dude with Dre, veteran of NWA, acting as the voice of reason. Eminem was inspired by a scene in *Animal House* in which one of the frat guys has the chance to take advantage of a comatose female student at a party, only for his angelic conscience to appear on one shoulder, with temptation in the form of the devil on the other. The spectacle of Dre piously espousing patience and temperance in his gruff, gangsta tones, as Slim Shady makes like a nerdy blowhard as he advocates all manner of vicious mayhem, is irresistible.

Over a flippant, head-bobbing keyboard backbeat, three scenarios are outlined by mix engineer Richard "Segal" Huredia. In the first, we meet Eddie, 23, whose life is going nowhere. He decides to cheer himself up by robbing a liquor store. At which point, Dr Dre announces himself as Eddie's "muthafucking conscience" and advises him to "think of the consequences" of his actions, warning him that the finger of shame will be pointed at him in the neighbourhood and urging him to have pity on the elderly store clerk, who's "older than George Burns".

Slim Shady, however, urges him to "Shoot that bitch! Are you that rich? Why you give a fuck if she dies?" before expressing his disappointment in the strangely angelic Dr Dre. In the second scenario, we meet Stan (the ill-fated "Stan" of The Marshall Mathers LP making an early appearance?), 21, who's contemplating spiking the drink of a 15-year-old girl he's met at a party and indulging in a spot of statutory rape. Again, Dre appears to warn Stan that it's unfair to take advantage of the girl, only for Slim Shady to egg him on to do the wrong thing: "Fuck that bitch right on the spot bare/ Till she passes out and she forgot how she got there."

Finally, there's Grady, a construction worker who comes back to his trailer to find his wife in bed with another man. Slim Shady advises summary homicide. "Cut this bitch's head off!" Again, Dre calls for restraint: ("What if there's an explanation for this shit?") At which point, Slim snaps and asks Grady if he's seriously going to take the advice of somebody who slapped Dee Barnes?

Having only known Dr Dre a few days, it's a tribute to Eminem's audacious cheek, as well as the understanding they'd struck up, that he laid this line on the ex-NWA producer, by his own account without warning. He was referring to an incident back in 1990 in which, following an appearance in the hip hop programme Pump It Up hosted by Dee Barnes, he accosted her at a Def Jam party, slammed her against the wall and pushed her down a flight of stairs. She would go on to sue him for $20 million, though the case was eventually settled out of court. He goes on to goad Dre further, "Mr NWA, Mr Straight Outta Compton" – for the somewhat prissy stand he has taken throughout this song. Indeed, in real life, Dre was making a conscious effort to put his rowdier, nastier days behind him as he took on the responsibilities of a hip hop executive. Significantly, he'd also issued two albums, including *The Firm*, in which he tried to sell a "cleaner", more grown-up version of himself to the world, to little commercial avail. "Guilty Conscience" is in part a mickey-take of this "new Dre".

Fortunately, Dre fell off his chair laughing when he heard the Dee Barnes line and, sportingly, dons the unlikely white robes required for the part of Conscience in this thoroughly entertaining and unsavoury (im)morality tale. Still, as if Slim's jeering is too much for him, he finally decides to jump shoulders and join the young devil. "Fuck it... what am I saying? Shoot 'em both, Grady, where's your gun at?" He'd make the same symbolic leap in his own career.

"Guilty Conscience" would be another massive hit for Eminem, in both America and Europe, receiving heavy airplay on rock as well as hip hop stations.

BRAIN DAMAGE

A song Eminem started between making *The Slim Shady EP* and the album of the same name, "Brain Damage" is one of the few songs that survived being thrown away in a fit of despondency at his apparently flagging career. It concerns one of the pivotal moments in his life – a terrible beating he took one wintry afternoon in 1983 at the hands of schoolmate D'Angelo Bailey, when he was a fourth grader. It seems that Marshall was involved in some sort of altercation with a friend of Bailey's when the latter rushed over and "hit me so hard into this snowbank I blacked out," according to Eminem himself.

Sent home, his ear began to bleed and he was taken to hospital, where he was diagnosed with a cerebral haemorrhage. He would spend the next few days in a coma, his brain severely swollen, with doctors not certain that he would survive.

The incident was the culmination of much bullying and harassment of young Marshall, who, perhaps because of his fast mouth, perhaps because of his odd, introverted nature, was a magnet for such torments during his school days – so much so that he took to feigning illness in order to get off school, something Eminem recreates with almost inappropriately comic gusto here.

The implication of "Brain Damage" is that this incident proved pivotal in the making of Marshall Mathers, left a permanent bolt of resentment and hatred in his neck, and made him the Frankenstein's monster he is today.

"Brain Damage" doesn't just speak volumes about Eminem but about the appeal of Eminem. Although he's a creature of hip hop, he's no strapping, medallion-clad gangsta *übermensch*, with a "bitch" on each arm, fanning 50-dollar bills in the faces of suckers and blasting away anyone who disrespects him. Neither, of course, are his audience. In "Brain Damage", he outlines frankly what he is, a bespectacled kid, a "corny looking white boy" with a chip on his shoulder because of the bullying he suffers, who's disrespectful to adults who do nothing to protect him, who's forced to take solace in petty acts of vengeance such as letting all the tyres down on the bike rack.

DR DRE AND EMINEM SHOW THEIR CONTEMPT FOR PHOTOGRAPHERS AT THE 1999 MTV VIDEO MUSIC AWARDS.

Then we get to the real beef of the song, in which Eminem goes so far as to name and shame his tormentor, "a fat kid named D'Angelo Bailey". In horribly traumatic detail, he recalls a pulverising he took while taking a piss in the urinals. Breathlessly packing in the syllables, he describes the blood soaking through his clothes, the choke-hold. Again, it's hard to think of anyone else in hip hop, black or white, who would share such a painful and degrading episode in their life with their audience.

However, fantasy and self-aggrandizement have always been essential components of hip hop and that's precisely what "Brain Damage" descends into from hereon in. First, the principal looks in on the scene and starts participating in the beating himself, before they leave him alone, assuming he's dead. Then, Eminem turns the tables, like Patricia Arquette in Tarantino's *True Romance*, grabbing whatever he can find in the bathroom – screws, sharp objects, brooms – seeking out the bully, repeatedly caving his head in, payback for all the niggling acts of oppression Eminem's suffered, from having his orange juice stolen to his tray tipped in the canteen.

Back home, Eminem's ear begins to bleed. His mom, who bears the brunt of the final verse's rage, is only concerned about the blood on her carpet and beats his head with a remote control. It falls to Eminem to retrieve the spilt contents of his cerebellum and sew them back up in his head. It speaks volumes about Eminem's simmering anger against his mother that he felt impelled to tack on this fictional finale.

In fact, Em's ever-litigious mother sued the school over the actual 1983 incident. The lawsuit filed suggested that, following the beating, her son suffered a variety of symptoms, including post-concussion syndrome, intermittent loss of hearing and "a tendency towards anti-social behaviour". The lawsuit, however, was dismissed.

As for D'Angelo Bailey, he was eventually tracked down by *Rolling Stone* among others. Working as a labourer, he still lived in the same Detroit neighbourhood where the incident took place, a chunky, soft-spoken family man who initially greeted his infamy with smiling bemusement. His own kids, he said, were into Eminem and he often signed autographs for young fans. He even asked for Em's telephone number.

However, none of this prevented Bailey from taking out a defamation lawsuit against Eminem, still ongoing in May 2003. He demanded a $1 million settlement, claiming that the song had caused him "anger and embarrassment". He also released a CD of his own, on which he threatened to mete out another dose of physical punishment to Eminem in the unlikely event that they met again.

IF I HAD

(See *The Slim Shady EP.*)

'97 BONNIE & CLYDE

(See *The Slim Shady EP.*)

ROLE MODEL

One of the first three songs he recorded with Dr Dre, "Role Model" sees Eminem spraying hyper-agitated bile every which way over a sleepily indifferent Dre loop. "I'm cancerous, so when I dis you wouldn't want to answer this," he warns, challenging the foolhardy to a smackdown on Jerry Springer if they dare to defy him. Such is the frame of mind Eminem pumps himself up to when he commits his words to paper. Someone famously described poetry as "emotion recollected in tranquillity". Eminem's "poetry" is emotion recollected, brooded on and warmed six times over until his head's set to explode. "My thoughts are so evil when I'm rhyming shit," he once said. "It's not how I feel in general, it's how I feel at the moment."

In this case, however, Eminem gets his rocks off with a comedic scattergun assault of late '90s celebrities. Among those who catch the hell are both Bill and Hillary Clinton ("I ripper her fuckin' tonsils out and fed her sherbet!"), Vanilla Ice and Lauryn Hill, whom Eminem suspects of disliking white people. "How the fuck can I be white, I don't even exist!" he responds here, as he slips into the convenient guise of the "non-existent" Slim Shady. Bill Clinton is dragged in as Eminem "confesses" to a drug habit. "If I said I never did drugs/That would mean I lie and get fucked more than the President does!" he argues, alluding to the hearing that followed Clinton's affair with intern Monika Lewinsky. Poor Sonny Bono, the recent tragic victim of a ski-ing accident, is not spared either. Em claims to "hit the trees harder" than the late pop star when he gets "too blunted off". Later, he claims co-responsibility for the murder of OJ Simpson's wife, Nicole, and for slapping Garth Brooks.

All of this namechecking, from Springer to Brooks, doesn't just confirm Eminem as an iconoclast with a lyrical paint-gun but is the sort of ear-catching topical stuff that confirms his own celeb status by proxy. Still, he's not above having a pop at more obscure targets in the hip hop world, such as Canibus (to whom he returned on *The Eminem Show*) and Cage, a New York rapper who claimed Eminem had ripped off his style. Em retorts that when he got Cage's tape, he didn't even listen to it, he dubbed over it.

Finally, yet another gratuitous, though possibly double-edged, whack at his mother, as he claims he's as "normal as Norman Bates" and apologizes to her for hitting her over the head with a shovel, the way Mrs Bates met her death in the prequel to Psycho.

All of this lurid tomfoolery is effectively designed to claim exemption from being commandeered as a "positive example" to young kids. It's a responsibility Eminem neither feels inclined nor qualified to live up to. But then, he protests, anyone who thinks anyone would be fool enough to emulate the excesses he depicts here is a fool themselves. "I'll tie a rope around my penis and jump from a tree/You probably want to grow up to be just like me!" he jeers, in his most scathing, sing-song sarcastic tones.

ON STAGE AT
THE UNIVERSAL
AMPHITHEATER,
LOS ANGELES 1999

MY FAULT

"Lounge", the skit that precedes "My Fault", is in fact its inspiration. Featuring Em and Marky and Jeff Bass from FBT Productions, they come

on like a bunch of rat pack crooners, bow ties off, in their cups, arms around each other, braying discordantly. "I didn't mean to... give you mushrooms." When Jeff Bass came up with the "mushrooms" line, Eminem got to thinking about an incident in which one of his friends had experienced a bad acid trip. "He was talking about how worthless he was and how fucked up his life was," recalled Eminem, who took it on himself to reassure the guy, who was going through a severe bout of depression.

Em comes out of this story rather well, being there for his pal, holding his hand in the dark times. It's significant, however, that for the purposes of this track he chooses to make the drugs victim a girl instead. In this fictional scenario, he's the bad guy, who's trying to cop off with Susan, introduced as "an ex-heroin addict" at some sleazy party. Telling her to "shut up" when she openly suspects his motives, he offers her a magic mushroom, only for the silly mare to scoff down practically the entire bag.

With Eminem going into panic mode, Susan starts hallucinating feverishly, rapping on how her father abused her, how she's a 26-year-old with no family or prospects, most of this addressed to a potted plant, before she mistakes Em for her own father. Em rushes off to find his friend Dave, who's taking a dump, before losing it completely, fading out on a chorus of whimpering apologies and anguished pleas to Susan to wake up.

Again, it's commendable for Eminem to drop the hip hop hardman persona and come on like a panicking, snivelling wreck. But still, those who suspect him of misogyny may have grounds for complaint here. Why couldn't he have told the story about another guy? Because the concern he (genuinely) expressed in the real-life situation here might seem a little, y'know, cissy.

So, make it a girl instead, lay a brisk ragga beat over the top to heighten the feeling of cartoon caper. Em does all the voices, including the girl, who sounds like one of the prissy airhead-types the comedian Sam Kinison used to mimic. Eminem's the one doing the apologizing here, over a chorus line borrowed from a fifties pop hit, "I Will Follow Him", but he's apologising for bringing the girl "into my world", naturally very much a man's world in which this naive, mushroom-gobbling-mess of a female has no hope of hacking it. So the joke's on her really, although her naivete doesn't quite square with her being an "ex-heroin addict".

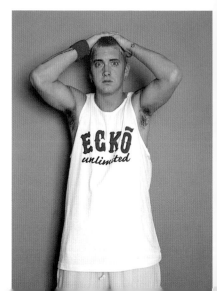

A cleaned up "Pizza Mix" of "My Fault" appeared on the 1999 Celebrity Death Match compilation album and it had also been considered as a single. However, it was decided that, following up "My Name Is" with another "goofy" type of track would have miscast Eminem as something of a novelty pop act in the public eye.

KEN KANIFF

Another skit, and another appearance for Eminem's regular character Ken Kaniff from Connecticut, a sleazy gay guy who propositions a snickering Em over the phone. The suggestion in "Cum On Everybody" is that Eminem himself adopts the Kaniff character for crank calls.

CUM ON EVERYBODY

Written between *The Slim Shady EP* and the *LP*, Eminem always intended this to be, as he announces, his "dance song". Musically, it's a gentle spoof of the sort of upholstered, bump'n'grind, poppy hip hop with which Puff Daddy and his ilk were busy making a fortune in the mid-'90s. The breathless, sultry chorus, "Come on everybody, get down tonight," is provided by the faithful Dina Rae. However, as is often the case with Eminem, the music bears little relationship to the verbal content – indeed, that's generally the point. "I thought, 'What if I make a dance song my way?'" said Eminem of this and the answer is, of course, that you end with something completely and perversely different.

There's another crack at Lauryn Hill ("I don't like white people!") and Kurt Cobain, to whom many people regarded Eminem as a white trash, blue-collar successor, but in whom Eminem was probably only interested for the gory lyrical grist provided by his bloody death, morbidly alluded to here. Freestyling cheerfully all over the place, with rhyme but not an awful lot of reason, he flips from bragging about having AIDS, to attempting suicide, to giving up rap altogether, to hanging out with "bitches" who mistake him for the Beastie Boys' Mike D, to nailing his foot down to the floorboard of his car out of sheer boredom.

For the benefit of those wondering where on earth he's going with this stuff, he informs us that he's "lost his mind" and is a "sick, sick bastard" who's "one Excedrin sandwich short of a medicine cabinet". However, even if he makes out otherwise on this exuberant but inessential outing, Eminem knows exactly what he's about, concluding cynically that "I only cuss to make your mom upset" – one of those lines Eminem says like he's saying it but doesn't really mean it but actually does mean it. Maybe. Such are the baffling, ironic flip-flops of his twisted mind.

ROCK BOTTOM

Cut from the same despondent cloth as "If I Had", "Rock Bottom" was intended, Eminem said, to be an uplifting song when he wrote it, a song intended to raise his own spirits, but the truth of just how low he felt at the time rises like oil to the surface. Over a wan backbeat faintly reminiscent of the Art Of Noise, the sort of soundtrack that usually accompanies the rueful loser in a Hollywood fadeout, Eminem mournfully dedicates the song to all the "happy" people who "have no idea what it's like to be broke as fuck".

Eminem did know that feeling – this, rather than his skin colour, was, he argued, the source of his "authenticity", that and the very real misery he had endured in his life.

Sure enough, at the time he was working on "Rock Bottom", Eminem was in the throes of a deep depression brought on by the ever-descending spiral of his circumstances. He was evicted from his house when it emerged that the flatmate to whom he'd been paying rent had been pocketing the money himself rather than paying the landlord. Furthermore, having seen the deadline he set himself to achieve a record deal expire, he almost expired himself following an overdose. He'd also recently lost his job. The very night he was recording vocals for this song, he took a handful of Codeine tablets which, luckily, he threw up before they could do him any serious damage.

The song looks at life from the other side of the hip hop telescope, life from the point of view of the impoverished "sucker MC" who has to sit and watch while other, less talented rappers than himself become overnight sensations. "It's cool to be the player but it sucks to be the fan," reflects Em. Although he's dirt poor, his daughter down to her last diaper, Eminem persists in exhibiting an ambivalent attitude towards money, which seduces and emasculates rap talent, causing "playa haters to turn bitch like they have vaginas," blinded and brainwashed by dollar signs, leaving your "ass mindless".

Still, "hungry, discouraged and malnourished", Eminem could do with a few dollar bills himself, in order to escape the miserable cycle of dead ends jobs, comfort drug consumption and crappy digs. When contemplating these realities, Eminem's eye for detail is superb, grabbing the emotional crux of the situation like a crotch. "My daughter wants to throw the ball but I'm too stressed to play…" is one line that stands out here.

Finally, Eminem seems to concede that he's going to make it out through exploiting the "evil" side of his nature, to become "backstabbing, deceitful and shady". Out of his mind with jealousy and desperation for a hip hop dream life of "women, money and fame", he ends the song on a note of hooded menace, turning to the listeners and looking us hungrily up and down with a mugger's eye: "Them rings look they got a few rocks on 'em." He sees himself turning to a life of crime, "running up on someone's lawn with guns drawn" and such is the cold, blazing intensity he brings to these rhymes that you can imagine that, had that tape not reached Dr Dre, this is precisely the kind of life to which he would have quite likely turned.

As it was, Eminem did turn "evil" in order to attain the success he craved, in the "backstabbing" and "shady" form of his reviled alter ego Slim, without whom Eminem would never have made his fortune.

JUST DON'T GIVE A FUCK

(See *The Slim Shady EP*.)

AS THE WORLD TURNS

Slim Shady is very much in harness on "As The World Turns", a double violent fantasy in which Eminem reveals an apparent contempt for generously-proportioned females. It's morally inexcusable stuff, of course, particularly the rape sequence, "redeemed" only by its sheer preposterousness and deranged inventiveness.

According to Em, the first verse of the song, which informs the second, was based on a long-time quarrel he had with a "fat chick" when he was back in school in gym class, whom he recalls as a "female bully". One suspects that the girl would have got much the better of her exchanges with the infant Eminem in real life, otherwise there'd be no festering need for the vengefulness of these lyrics. Here, Eminem reinvents himself as a junior psychopath, the blame once again laid on his mother who "took my bike away". Duly tipped over the edge, young Em roasts his guinea pig in a microwave, slaps his teachers and masturbates in front of

counsellors. Then, when he gets into a fight with the fat girl in gym class, he is transformed, Incredible Hulk-style, and hurls her into the swimming pool below.

A lyrical interlude follows in which Eminem beefs at US hip hop magazine *The Source* for the 2-rating of his last album, then tosses off the best lines of the song, though it's completely unconnected with the rest of it. "We drive around in million dollar sports cars/While little kids hide this tape from their parents like bad report cards." The "million dollar" bit is knowingly absurd and exaggerated, while the second line shows that Eminem was under none of the cosy illusions stars often entertain about the make-up of their fanbase or what became of his stuff when it was released into the world.

A LIVE PERFORMANCE IN 2000.

The final verse is a grotesque and repulsive caper, partly recreated in cartoon form on the sleeve, in which Eminem screws to death a fat woman he picks up at a laundromat; indirect vengeance for the taunting of an overweight little girl many years ago back in Junior High. The song concludes, over a slightly cheap and tacky FBT production, with Eminem sermonizing like some travelling preacher about the "small obstacles and challenges every day" that "we must go through". It's this sort of comic framing which makes it nigh-impossible to keep a straight face while castigating Slim Shady for his many sins.

I'M SHADY

Eminem originally wrote this over a Sade track, before coming across Curtis Mayfield's "Pusherman", via Ice-T's own sample of it on "Power". He unabashedly lifts the chorus straight from Mayfield on this, one of the more musically pleasing offerings on *The Slim Shady LP*. "I'm Shady" shuffles along to a sugary, laid-back groove as the ever-volatile Eminem flits back and forth between his personae and revisits some now-familiar obsessions – AIDS, suicide (he brags that he doesn't want a normal death, he wants to "die twice"), his rampant inadequacy as a role model for kids. He goes into a long, derisive spiel about liking "happy" things – birds, bees, things that make him "happy and gleeful – like when my teacher sucked my wee wee in pre-school." A fib, of course, but clearly, Eminem regards the very concept of innocence itself as a fairytale, a lie, having been robbed of his own so early on in his life.

In Shady mode, Em temporarily abandons hip hop conventions and actually brags of being a plagiarist, rather than accusing others of it ("Six months later you hear your lyrics on my shit"). The end result is the same, however – to piss off other MCs. Then, despite a chorus line in which he comes on like Curtis's despicable pusher, plying acid, mushrooms, weed, Eminem offers a more truthful inventory of his bad habits, which seem relatively moderate by Shady standards. A few pills, some weed, beer – but he steers clear of crack, smack, speed and cocaine. Oh, and while he's on the subject, he didn't really kill Kim and he probably hasn't got AIDS, although he can't be certain as he's "too scared to get tested".

None of this is intended to keep us guessing but to impress on us yet again that Eminem is messing with our minds, sometimes kidding, sometimes deadly serious.

BAD MEETS EVIL

A collaboration, this, with fellow Detroit rapper Royce Da 5-9, with whom Eminem had previously worked on an EP of the same name, "Bad Meets Evil" is topped and tailed by Eminem coming on like some toothless old-timer spinning yarns of the old Wild West out on the porch; yarns of Shady and Royce, the "quickest damn gun slingers I've ever seen" who were killed in cold blood, shot in the back like Billy The Kid. This, though, only gives the chance to come on all supernatural on us, because now Shady is a "ghost trapped in a beat", transmitting his voice through the head of Royce.

With its wheezy fuzzbox and tingling Godfather-style guitar accompaniments, it's hard to take "Bad Meets Evil" too seriously. Rather it's a good-natured, albeit seriously ill bout of verbal jousting between two rappers who are clearly thick as thieves. Royce goes up first, challenging Eminem to a duel whereby they come at each other in fast cars to "see who'll swerve first." Having tastefully compared him and Em to the "Nazis" trying to take over the earth and casually alluding to "burying the Christ corpse in my past life", the mic passes to Eminem, who delivers the chorus; he and Royce have smoked so much weed they "look like Vietnamese people". More violent and occasionally nonsensical pyrotechnics from Royce, one moment murdering his own soul, the next dodging bullets, Matrix-style, then back to Eminem, who steals the track with a distinctive example of his rap virtuosity, hitting repeatedly on the long "e" syllable, – "I breathe ether in three lethal amounts… stab myself in the knee, releasing rage…".

Only when Em states he's bad "like Steven Segal" does he stink up the track a little. Segal might have seemed hot at the time but here's an example of the danger of topical pop-cultural allusions – they're liable to date horribly on you. Segal went from bad to plain bad within a few years.

STILL DON'T GIVE A FUCK

Eminem's manager Paul Rosenberg came up with the idea that Eminem should record a sequel to "Just Don't Give A Fuck", presumably in case anyone should be wondering if there had been any movement in Eminem's mind on the topic since the first track. Needless to say, there was not. "This is me," said Eminem. "Ima be it an Ima stay that way."

Against the sound of heavy rainfall, Eminem makes his final address to us, with cinematic portentousness, as if delivering an epilogue in the closing scene. People ask him if he's afraid of death; people think all kinds of "retarded shit" of him, that he worships the devil, for instance. In a bit of cleft thinking, Eminem doesn't try to clear his name of these absurd charges but rather protests that he cannot change his own nature. "If I offended you? Good. 'Cause I still don't give a fuck."

After a defiant, high-speed, lyrical chase, running amok with guns and knives, spiritual reality sets in as Eminem depicts himself as worn out and uncertain of his fate, ducking down as he writes the rhyme in case he gets

struck by lightning. In the press notes to *The Slim Shady LP*, Eminem had (self-dramatizingly) remarked, in the light of Tupac Shakur's fate, that he may not be around on the planet that long himself. Still, that didn't mean he was riven with regret or remorse. In an air-punching, singalong chorus he celebrates all the drugs he's done, the people he's offended and, while he admits he misses his past, concludes "I still don't give a fuck, you can kiss my ass!"

The rest of the song is a mixture of whacked-out, all-conquering braggadocio in which he namechecks Saddam Hussein and luridly compares himself to a hybrid of Charles Manson, "horrorcore" Detroit rapper Esham and Ozzy Osbourne. Characteristically, however, this all runs parallel with more frank reflections and navel-gazing anxiety. Even now, to his astonishment, he still has money worries. He claims to be experiencing drug withdrawal symptoms. He worries if he's exhausted his creative wells, how much more he can say ("I can't rap any more – I done murdered the alphabet"). He describes himself as a loner, a one-man posse.

He even eschews the promiscuous lifestyle supposedly enjoyed by hip hoppers, yearning rather for domestic stability. Well, that's a charitable way of putting it. As Eminem puts it, "I don't rap to get the women – fuck bitches/Give me a fat slut that cooks and does dishes." And, in lines which faintly recall the existential despondency of that other white trash superstar, Kurt Cobain, he complains, "I don't know why the fuck I'm here in the first place/My worst day on this earth was my first birthday." The song fades out to a guitar loop, which chimes eerily like a music box.

All of which inflects and deflects what initially comes on like the crude, boorish triumphalism of the chorus. This is more than a giant flip of the bird. This is the masked cry of a poisoned, angry, lonely and confused soul at his wit's end. Still, at least *The Slim Shady LP* would offer him the small consolation of turning him from dirt poor to filthy rich practically overnight.

THE MARSHALL MATHERS LP

The success of *The Slim Shady LP* naturally afforded Eminem a financial security that had supposedly been the stuff of his dreams. He was given a hero's welcome on returning to Detroit and the Mayor gladly shook hands with the city's freshest son. Yet he held fast to some of the scepticism about fame which had characterised "Rock Bottom". He was withering about the sudden fawning treatment he received when he went to clubs, the memory of a time when these people would have kept him on the wrong side of the velvet rope still raw. "Now I've got people clearing tables for me."

In photos of the numerous awards ceremonies he attended throughout 1999, he looks grim and noncommittal, holding up the double finger to fans and photographers as if they were set that way in an invisible splint. He took a little time out with daughter Hailie but then went straight back to work. Over the summer, he filled in for Cypress Hill on the Vans Warped tour, before hauling his own ass, plus members of his posse D12, on the road, filling venues across the US and later Europe. Among those joining him onstage were Dr Dre and even Dustin Hoffman, who took the part of the dancing Mummy at a show at LA's Coliseum.

Having hitherto eschewed the sort of guest cameos that generally litter hip hop albums, Em was all over other people's material in 1999, including Dr Dre's *The Chronic*, Missy Eliot's *Da Real World* and the *Wild Wild West* soundtrack. He set up his own record label, Shady Records. He picked up a brace of MTV and Grammy Awards. No rest for the wicked.

On the home front, however, Eminem's life was turning into the bizarre stuff of daytime TV shows. Despite "97' Bonnie & Clyde", despite being depicted dead in the trunk of a car on the front of *The Slim Shady LP*, Kim married Eminem in June 1999. "I've always taken his word on things and stood by his side," she declared, in a rare interview, in which she expressed

EMINEM PICKS UP YET ANOTHER MTV VIDEO AWARD.

the faithful, if staggeringly misguided, hope that "Just because my husband is an entertainer doesn't mean that our personal business is for everyone's entertainment purposes." They would continue to live in Em's Mother's trailer, Mrs Mathers-Briggs having moved out to Kansas City.

It was Mrs Mathers-Briggs, however, who would drop the biggest bomb of the year, when on September 17, she filed a $10 million lawsuit against her own son for defamation of character, following Em's crack on "My Name Is" about her dope smoking. She claimed to have suffered stress, humiliation and anxiety, with Fred Gibson, her lawyer, suggesting that Eminem had deliberately exaggerated his childhood privations, trading in his dear mom's reputation and good name for some street cred. Mrs Mathers-Briggs claimed that she had raised Eminem in a drugs-free environment and that if she had been guilty of anything, it had been in protecting him too much.

Eminem was appalled, though apparently not entirely surprised, by the lawsuit. "My mom's crazy," he scoffed, delivering a welter of counter-claims – that his mother had charged $20 a time to be photographed with fans, that she had auctioned off Eminem's posters to local kids after he'd left to go on tour.

Meanwhile, a feud with fellow Detroiters the "horrorcore" outfit Insane Clown Posse was brewing, which dated back to 1995, over accusations that Eminem had used their name on one of his flyers to attract more punters to one of his shows. "I don't want to pay the studio time even to diss them," said Eminem on an MTV phone-in show. Yet that's exactly what he would do on the Marshall Mathers LP.

And then, at the end of 1999, Eminem found himself facing a suit not only from his mother but also from his grandmother, Betty Kresin, who was unhappy at his plans to sample a track recorded by his Uncle Ronnie. She was unclear about her specific motives for the suit but described her grandson's music as "garbage" and Em himself as a "bitter boy" who was "angry and disrespectful" towards her. On this one, Eminem backed down.

And so, weighed down with all of these tribulations, as well as the accolades and brickbats of 1999 (including the friendly but wounding suggestion by MTV's Kurt Loder, in a face-to-face interview, that some of his lyrics were just a tad homophobic), Eminem entered the recording studio in November. The mooted title of the album would make it clear that Slim Shady would take a backseat for this ride. There would be less of the zany psychopathology, less of the flip, x-rated homicidal capers. This time, Em promised, the album would be about the "real" Eminem – Marshall Mathers – and the black psychic tar that made him what he was, made him say and do the things he said and did. This was the real story of Eminem and it promised to be heavier, and nastier, than even his sickest fantasy spiels.

Once again, Dr Dre would be in on the act, producing five of the album's tracks and mixing five others. He described the Dre/Eminem modus operandi as follows. "We get in there, get bugged out, stay in the studio for fuckin' two days. Then you wake up, pop the tape in, like, 'Let me see what I've done.'"

With The Marshall Mathers LP, coupled with the events of 1999, it was no longer possible to be curtly dismissive of Eminem as a Caucasian, post-modern pop chancer masquerading as a badass hip hopper. Lawyer Fred Gibson's assertion that Eminem would soon be exposed as a white middle class boy from a well-heeled background looked increasingly lame. Unless this whole business with his family was some elaborate, World Wrestling Federation-style set-up, you could see the mess this boy's life was in, had always been in. Eminem was not pop. Indeed, he was beyond the usual pale of hip hop.

And, on The Marshall Mathers LP, he would not only cut a hip hop album that was among the genre's "illest" in every sense of the word,

MISSY ELLIOT HAS WORKED WITH AND DEFENDED EMINEM WHO HAS OFTEN BEEN ACCUSED OF MISOGYNY.

he'd cut himself open and let it bleed all over the album. This wasn't just a grim autopsy on the state of modern celebrity but an exposure of the deep wells of collective anger and simmering, impotent frustration that Eminem had tapped into among the young (often very young) and the pissed off (often very pissed off), and that had made him perhaps the most disturbing superstar of our time, the ultimate anti-celebrity. On "The Real Slim Shady" he describes his core constituency – guys just like him, flipping burgers, flipping the finger.

The Marshall Mathers LP would spark a highbrow debate concerning the morality of Eminem; whether his apparent spewings of misogyny and homophobia could be excused under the banner of art; whether the right to free speech allowed for this sort of incitement to hatred; whether Eminem was a genius, evil, or an evil genius. It would trigger an alliance of far leftist groups (including feminists and gay rights organisations) with right wing, pro-censorship groups of the wash-your-mouth-out-with-soap-and-water variety. Once again, anyone who imagined that this sort of furore would douse the flames of Eminemania was sadly mistaken. The album had sold upward of six million copies by the end of the year. The genius was out of the bottle.

PUBLIC SERVICE ANNOUNCEMENT

A reprise of the announcement that opens *The Slim Shady LP,* this one is rather more forthright. Here we are cordially invited to suck Slim Shady's cock if we find this album not to our taste and that, furthermore, our statutory rights are very much affected by purchasing *The Marshall Mathers LP.* For in agreeing to do so, we have "just kissed [Slim's] ass. Furthermore, Slim is "fed up with your shit and he is going to kill you." Whereupon Eminem is invited to say a few words, which are as follows: "Yeah. Sue me."

Any hope that we are in for an album of tender MOR ballads is thus expunged at the outset.

KILL YOU

Eminem comes roaring out of the traps in Slim Shady mode, with one of his fastest, funniest and most furious raps to date; rasping, unshaven, paranoid and taking on all comers, with a pitbull growl replacing the slightly adenoidal whine of the previous album. Over a halting, ragga-tinged backbeat with a touch of Sesame Street about it, Eminem once again takes us right back to the source of his mess, his early childhood, in which, he says, his mother lied to him about his missing father having been such an asshole. All along, it turns out, she was the crazy one and there was nothing he could do about it, except fester and mutate into the monster he is today.

Admitting he "can't rap about being broke no more", Eminem works himself up into hysteria, in which bits of his life over the past year pop up like bits of undigested food in a spew of vomit – his appearance on the *Rolling Stone* cover for one, as well as a disastrous appearance on a Sunday college radio show in which the presenter, Sister Tamu, had pulled him off the air when he started freestyling profanely. He's scornful of radio shows who invite him on to argue "because their ratings stink". The frenzy reaches

INSANE CLOWN POSSE – FELLOW DETROIT RAPPERS WERE INVOLVED IN A FEUD WITH EMINEM UNTIL 2005.

an early pitch of v-shaped virtuosity as he spits, "I invented violence, you vile, venomous, volatile, vicious Vain Vicadi, vrinnn, Vrinn VRINNN,". "Bitches, wives, nuns, sluts" are the object of his scattergun, murderous ire, running through the verses like a psychotic dervish, brandishing whatever sharp objects he can lay his hands on, including "OJ [Simpson]'s machete".

Clearly, however, Eminem is asserting his right to shoot his mouth off rather than endorsing mass gender-cide. This "death threat" is intended as a counterblast to those who wish to silence him, including, worryingly, the "faggots" who keep egging him on. Eminem had explained to MTV's Kurt Loder that his use of the word "faggot" was not homophobic but meant something more like "softy" and seemed genuinely horrified that anyone might have thought otherwise.

Amid all the 90mph wordplay, the measured delivery of the chorus, the first hook Eminem came up with for this song, is one of the funniest moments in its thuggish bathos. "You don't wanna – fuck with Sha-dy" seems all primed and set up for a real pithy couplet, but what you get instead is, "'Cause Sha-dy – will fuckin' kill you."

Finally, having chased the un-named "bitch" (not his mother) through to the end and having her at knifepoint, Eminem concludes the song with a chuckle. "I'm just playing, ladies, you know I love you," he says, though if anything, this only serves to add insolent salt to the song's imaginary flesh wounds. Eminem correctly described "Kill You" as "ridiculous", the more so because by tacking on his disclaimer at the end, he could say whatever he wanted beforehand.

STAN

After the teasing of "Kill You", Eminem gets more serious and soul-searching than he'd ever been with "Stan", a contender for his greatest song. It starts up with a distant sample of Dido's misty and subdued "Thank You", which Eminem had received on a tape from the DJ the 45 King. Then, following an ominous cinematic thunderclap that warns us this tale is going to end in tears, Eminem plays the part of his own, most ardent fan, Stan. The first letter he writes to him, addressed to "Slim", is adulatory, but right from the get-go alarm bells start to jingle. You know this guy is a little unhinged, wants to get too close for comfort. He left his cell, pager and home phone number on the previous letter and can't figure out why "Slim" hasn't called him back yet. Clearly some problem at the post office.

Turns out "Stan" feels he has a lot in common with Em. He, too, has a wife, a child on the way. He commiserates with him over the death of his Uncle Ronnie – he had a friend commit suicide on him too. Stan's four walls are covered with Eminem posters which he stares at all day, seeing both the superstar and himself reflected in them.

The next letter ratchets up the tension. Stan's pissed off that Em still hasn't been in touch. Meanwhile, the star's made the further mistake of giving Stan's six-year old brother the brush-off after they stood outside one of his concerts for four hours, waiting for an autograph. This curt act of negligence, probably instantaneously forgotten by the superstar, wounds Stan gravely.

He takes everything Em says and does to heart, this worst of all. It turns out he met Eminem, back in Denver in the early days, when it was still possible to get close to him, when Em made him a promise: "You said if I'd write you, you'd write back."

Even now he has faith in him, as well as tattoos of him all over his body, which he cuts up incidentally, the blood-rush "like adrenalin", the extreme mark of an obsessive. (Those who indulge in self-harm are often said to be compensating for a lack of any sense of control or destiny in their lives. Their own bodies are the last thing, the one thing, of which they are in charge.) Stan has no life of his own anymore, and is looking to merge with Eminem's, a dangerous form of empathy. "My girlfriend's jealous 'cause I talk about you 24/7 /But she don't know you like I know you, Slim, no one does…"

The third communiqué is via cassette. Needless to say, Eminem still hasn't returned his letter and with this final betrayal, Stan loses it completely. "All I wanted was a lousy letter or a call!" Even now, however, as he slides towards oblivion, he does it Eminem-style, careering aimlessly and drunkenly down the road at 90mph in his car. He sarcastically quotes back at him the line from "My Name Is": "I drank a fifth of vodka – want to dare me to drive?" But that's just what he's gone and done, plus he's taken "1000 downers" and it's all Eminem's fault. "I hope your conscience eats at you!"

But it gets worse. There's a scream: "Shut, up, bitch, I'm trying to talk!" He's bundled his pregnant girlfriend into the trunk, "97' Bonnie & Clyde " style. He plunges into the water, his last thought how he's going to send out the cassette now that he's dead, cruelly revealing him as a dimwit as well as a psycho.

Now, belatedly, Eminem writes back, hip, measured and tactfully, suggesting that he's some experience in talking down the sort of hotheads he's plagued by when the need arises. He meant to write sooner; he "didn't mean to diss you". He's sorry he didn't see him at the show, here's that autograph for his little brother. But then he reaches out further, gets beyond just being polite. "What's this shit you said about you like to cut your wrists too?/ I say that shit just clowning, dogg – c'mon, how fucked up is you?" But it's too late. As Eminem reminisces about a story he heard recently about some guy who drove his car off a bridge, killing his wife, girlfriend and unborn child, the penny finally drops and he ends with a chastened and uncharacteristically mild profanity: "Damn".

One of the many amazing things about "Stan" is that it seems to represent a turnaround in Eminem's thinking. Hitherto, he's always insisted, with derisive gusto, that his fans should be credited with some intelligence, that none of them are going to go out and do the things Slim Shady does like a rabid pack of Pavlovian hounds. Yet here Eminem imagines, in one of the most grippingly lucid, concentrated and coherent narratives in all rap music, that this is precisely what could happen, with devastating consequences.

As his fan base multiplied rapidly beyond a local cult following, he would have been as much prey to the crazed element that stalks the fringes of celebrity as anyone in the public eye. In fact, even more so, given the feelings that he tapped into. And certainly, throughout the "Eminem" years, there have been recorded cases of Eminem fans doing terrible, Eminem-style things. In 2001, it was reported that one David Hurcombe, a 17-year-old student who threw himself in front of a train, included lyrics from Eminem's "Rock Bottom" in his suicide note, while in 2002, an Eminem and D12 fan was sentenced to life imprisonment for beating to death a homeless man, having repeatedly listened to the D12 track "Fight Music". Clearly, the evidence of connections with these sorts of acts is flimsy and, as Eminem says to Stan, these were people who doubtless "had issues". Yet the very fact that he sat down to write "Stan" suggests that Eminem had paused for thought to consider that he might have some sort of responsibilities to his audience.

Another way of looking at "Stan", however, is that this is Eminem contemplating his old self (he plays Stan in the video) and what he might have made of Eminem the superstar while he was still living in Shitty Street.

Stan, in this scenario, represents all the Eminems that didn't make it, who experienced the same problems and frustrations as he did but didn't have either the talent, intelligence or fortune to find a way out of their circumstances. This is Eminem trying to talk to them, modifying the "kiss my ass" line he'd followed in "I Just Don't Give A Fuck". Here, he's a little troubled at how far he's come, how far away he is from where he was at before. Certainly, there isn't another song in pop, rock or hip hop which addresses so honestly and full-frontally the most awkward questions concerning the relationship between the star and the fan.

The use of Dido's "Thank You" isn't particularly lyrically apposite. It's a paean to her boyfriend, yet it sits perfectly in the background of "Stan", adding a soulful and ruminative backdrop to the deadly build-up of the narrative. Such was the measure of Eminem's star pulling power at this time, however, that thanks to being sampled by him, Dido went from being the obscure sister of Faithless's Rollo to the world's highest-earning female singer-songwriter practically overnight. She appeared in the video for "Stan", bound and gagged in the trunk of the car, and took a nasty headwound against the car jack in the process. However, although a little intimidated by Eminem's reputation, she got on famously with him. "Within a minute we were having a laugh and taking the piss out of each other. People confuse him with the characters in his songs. But it's like Stephen King. He does some scary shit and it's warped beyond belief. But it's not real. I got close enough to Eminem to know that he's not misogynistic or homophobic."

WHO KNEW

Having stared at his own reflection in the dark waters of "Stan", on this track Eminem asserts himself, over a Dr Dre-produced, hopscotch backbeat and synth string loop. You think he's to blame for the stupid and dangerous things kids do? "Don't blame me when Li'l Eric jumps off the terrace. You should have been watching him – apparently you ain't parents." On "Who Knew", the spotlight's on mom and dad, movie heroes like Arnold Schwarzenegger, the authorities, including the incumbent of the highest office in the land. "You want me to fix up lyrics while the president gets his dick sucked?" he scoffs, another reference to President Clinton's dalliance with Monica Lewinsky, which had shattered the White House's capacity to give the nation a moral lead.

Eminem's message is simple. You think I'm screwed? You think I'm screwing with your kids? Look around you. Kids don't learn about swearing from Eminem records. They learn about it in the schoolyard, from the school bus driver, the same as he did. Uncles are happy to take their little nephews to see gun-toting action movies, yet they want to censor Eminem's far less graphic and SFX-heavy raps on the same subject. "Take drugs, rape sluts, make fun of gay clubs," says Eminem, but only to demonstrate that these are just words, "for your kids' amusement". Then: "Damn! How much damage can you do with a pen?"

As for Eminem himself, he's not carrying out a masterplan. He's as shocked at his own success as everyone else. "A couple of years ago I was more poor than you are." He's barely had time to make sense of his own rise to fame, the consequences of which he can't be responsible for.

As ever with Eminem in full ranty mode, he slips all over the place, breaking off to have a gratuitous kick at the corpse of poor Sonny Bono and a pop at Christopher Reeve before returning to harangue his tormentors. He boasts that "I don't do black music, I don't do white music, I make fight music for high school kids." That the "fight school" reference, as already mentioned regarding "Stan", was taken up by a young Englishman as the

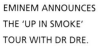

EMINEM ANNOUNCES THE 'UP IN SMOKE' TOUR WITH DR DRE.

63

cue to beat a homeless man to death does leave an unfortunate, retrospective hole in Eminem's argument here. However, the overall point of "Who Knew" – "Get aware, wake up, get a sense of humour/Quit trying to censor music," is well taken. Ban Eminem because of one psychopath and you'd be banning The Beatles' *White Album* because of Charles Manson's twisted take on it as well.

STEVE BERMAN

One of the funnier skits, this, as Eminem takes a roasting from Interscope exec Steve Berman, played by himself, over the new album. In pops Eminem, all bushy-tailed, expecting a pat on the back, when Berman lays it on him: "This album is selling less than nothing! Tower Records told me to shove this record up my ass! I'm gonna lose my fucking job over this!" Then he kicks a humbled Eminem, who's not been able to get a word in edgeways, out of his office. Eminem could afford to laugh at himself, especially since the reality of *The Marshall Mathers LP* turned out to be exactly the opposite of everything it's presented as in this skit. Did Eminem ever for one moment think it would be otherwise? In his most paranoid moments, possibly.

CHRISTINA AGUILERA WAS THE LYRICAL TARGET OF ONE OF EMINEM'S MANY GRUDGES.

THE WAY I AM

If "Stan" isn't Eminem's greatest ever moment, that may be because "The Way I Am" is. Musically, it was conceived by Eminem alone – a simple, three-note loop, wheeling through the song like a sawn-off Bach motif, with bells tolling with Gothic morbidity in the background.

"The Way I Am" was conceived by Eminem in what began in a fit of pique but then grew up into a gigantic, ulcerous rant against everything and anybody, including his fans. Stan had his turn a couple of tracks back but now Eminem rails at the obsessives invading his space so that "I can't take a shit in the bathroom/Without someone standin' by it/No I won't sign your autograph!"

Written at his in-laws' house, "The Way I Am" was borne from the grief Eminem felt he was getting from his record company to come up with another monster pop smash to match "My Name Is". Added to that nagging frustration were the lawsuit from his mother, and the reappearance of his father in his life, anxious to make up for lost time. Then, he was told that the reference to the Columbine massacre, which he'd intended for the song "I'm Back", would have to be toned down. He'd already had the video for "Guilty Conscience" chopped to bits in the moral panic that surrounded the high school killing. In his own way anticipating film maker Michael Moore's *Bowling For Columbine*, which lambasted the misplaced hysteria surrounding the infamous high school massacre, Eminem wondered at the hypocrisy that deemed that this tragedy and not others was considered sacrosanct. "People die in the city all the time," he observed, indignantly. "People get shot, stabbed, raped, mugged, killed and all kinds of shit."

All of this grief, much of it coming from the people who were supposed to be on his side (his family, friends, fans, censoring him, smothering him, leeching on him), set the vein pumping purple in Eminem's temple and resulted in this magnificent yell of primal boiling fury. And it's controlled fury – there's a discipline, the way he hits every third note, which helps him to channel the rage.

Em kicks off in a dense cloud of weed, reflecting on the downside of being the "meanest MC on this earth", who's "cursed with this curse to just curse". (Eminem once speculated that he was a victim of Tourette's Syndrome!) But then, in a sustained growl that's a million miles away from Slim Shady's nerdy, evil impishness, he starts poking us in the chest. First, it's the fans who approach him in the street when he's trying to feed his daughter. "I don't KNOW you and NO I don't OWE you a MOTHer-fucking – thing/I'm NOT Mr NSync." Warning us that his "tank is on empty", and on the point of violence, he laughs off the threat of a lawsuit. He'll smile, "buy you a wardrobe", it's nothing to him, just get out of his face.

He admits he "can be a prick", he "doesn't mean to be mean", but then, as he puts it in a chorus which recoils smartly into a coy ambivalence at odds with the directness of the verses, "I am whatever you say I am/If I wasn't, why would you say I am?/In the paper, the news, every day I am," before levelling the eyebrow-raising complaint that, "Radio won't even play my jam" – or not in its uncensored form, at any rate.

Once you untangle the sarcasm, it seems Eminem is saying, 'You want me to be the bad guy? That's what you buy into? Fine. Because believe me, I can be the bad guy."

65

Following a strange reference to his father, whom he never knew, Em concentrates his ire on the media, who point the finger of blame at him for society's ills, only for Eminem to flip one right back. He sails in to defend Marilyn Manson, whom he'd gently lampooned on "My Name Is" but whom he now regarded as a fellow scapegoat. How ridiculous, he screams, that the Columbine massacre was blamed on Marilyn: "WHERE WERE THE PARENTS AT?" He casts a wider eye over middle America ("it's a tragedy") but stops short of social analysis, quickly getting back to his persecuted self. Even now, however, Eminem has a moment of lucidity. This may all be bullshit but it's bullshit of a sort that his angry muse subsists on, that "feeds me the fuel that I need for the fire."

Then, in the last verse, Eminem addresses the issue that triggered this bout of stress in the first place – record company pressure for him to come up with another "My Name Is". He admits he's "not going to be able to top" that single, but then protests that nor should he try to, why should he need to, if it means he'll merely be reduced to some "pop sensation" angling for MTV prominence. Finally, one last time, he scotches the "wigger" accusations, the bulk of which, he claims, come not from blacks but from "cocky Caucasians" ceaselessly and repeatedly interrogating him like a rap POW. Screw them. "It seems like white magazines such as *Spin* and *Rolling Stone* focus on my whiteness more than black magazines," Eminem had complained to *Vibe* magazine.

"The Way I Am" is Eminem at the absolute peak of his form – warty, obnoxious, exasperating, exasperated, righteous, inconsistent, scaldingly acute, hanging way out there at the end of his tether. He's so angry you think he might spontaneously combust. You can practically feel the phlegm in your face as he harangues you. The public took their punishment gratefully. Coupled with a video featuring daughter Hailie and Marilyn Manson, hovering behind Eminem like some Gothic shadow, the single was one of Eminem's biggest to date, rebranding him in the public mind as a meaner, more rounded, substantial and "4 real" figure than the smartass X-rated peccadilloes of "My Name Is" had suggested.

THE REAL SLIM SHADY

He's a contrary boy, Eminem. Having just rapped angrily on "The Way I Am" about how "My Name Is" was a one-off that he'd never top and in any case would never want to top as he didn't want to go pop, what does he serve up next? "The Real Slim Shady" is every bit as poppy and fizzily infectious as "My Name Is", a calculated, direct hit which he and Dre spent hour after solid studio hour trying to dream up, before Em's ears pricked up at a doodling riff played by Dre's keyboard player Tommy Coster Jr. After a few adjustments, they finally had the pop hook the record company had been screaming at them to deliver.

Now, Eminem had the weekend to come up with the single. Fortunately, inspiration was close at hand. Em had been brooding about remarks Will Smith had made at the MTV Music Awards, at which both artists had been present. When accepting his award, Smith had observed that he didn't need swear words to sell his records and took a swipe at gangsta rappers for their over-reliance on expletives. Eminem took these comments as pointing at him, as a personal diss. "Not everybody is as happy as Will Smith," Eminem later said. "So if he sees life as being about birds and bees and flowers let him rap about birds and bees and flowers but don't diss anybody else… I felt he was taking a stab at me and Dre and anybody who uses profanity to express themselves."

The second incident was when Christina Aguilera, during an appearance on MTV with Carston Daly and Fred Durst, had made what might seem a relatively innocuous remark to the effect that Eminem seemed pretty cute but that she thought he was married to Kim. Eminem was married to Kim but he didn't especially want the fact to be broadcast at that point, and was enraged at what he saw as Ms Aguilera's snickering indiscretion. Aguilera also went on to advise female MTV viewers to "not let your man disrespect you", as she felt Em had Kim, a follow-up point which spectators of this spat often disregarded and Eminem himself never really addressed.

Both these incidents demonstrated Eminem's Olympic-standard ability to bear a grudge and he comes back at both Smith and Aguilera with both barrels blazing on "The Real Slim Shady". On Smith; "Will Smith don't gotta cuss in his raps to sell records? Well I do, so fuck him and fuck you too!" (Ironically, for its first two verses at least, "The Real Slim Shady" is relatively "cuss-lite" by Eminem standards.) On Aguilera; "I should download her audio on MP3/And show the world how you gave Eminem VD!"

His attack on Aguilera broadens here to take in Britney Spears and all the "boy and girl bands" then prevalent in American pop who were anaemic anathema to Eminem. He would carry his feud with Spears and Aguilera well into 2000, bringing blow-up dolls named after the two of them onstage and simulating sex with them. (In the video for "The Real Slim Shady", Em also dresses up as Britney Spears and again features a Christina Aguilera blow-up doll.) These attacks on manufactured teenypop seemed gratuitous to some. However, they came at a time when the sugary stuff was threatening to supersaturate the entire music scene. As *Rolling Stone*'s David Fricke observed, "The US pop industry is obsessed with the teenage market. Even our magazine regularly covers groups like the Backstreet Boys and N'Sync. Eminem seems to be about the last stand against all the homogeneity."

Indeed, one of the various themes threading through "The Real Slim Shady" is the satisfaction he took that an "army of me" was developing in the USA. "There's a million if us just like me/Who cuss like me, who just don't give a fuck like me."

Although the chorus cuffs "All you other Slim Shadys" who are "just imitating", Eminem drew a clear distinction between the aspiring Eminem "career"-wannabes in the pop and hip hop market itself, and the regular fans out there who simply identified with him. He happily attended Eminem lookalike pageants and fan gatherings, allowing himself to be photographed alongside dozens of peroxided would-be doppelgangers.

And when in the chorus he demands, "Won't the real Slim Shady please stand up?" it's as if he's bidding for a moment akin to that in Kubrick's *Spartacus* when one by one the captured slaves shout "I'm Spartacus". They're not, of course, but there's a bit of him in all of them – much as Eminem chuckles at the end here, "Guess there's a Slim Shady in all of us." It might be, he says, the pissed-off guy who works in Burger King spitting in your food, or the guy letting off steam riding his car around in circles, music blasting out of his stereo.

Amid all of this are some very funny asides, including Eminem imagining himself so burnt out at age 30 that he's put in a nursing home, still horny as ever but unable to rise to the occasion even after consuming a whole bag of Viagra. The outtro, featuring what sounds like someone in the very early stages of learning to play the recorder, sets the seal on what's a brief return to the ultra-flippant Eminem of old.

REMEMBER ME?

One of the minor tracks on *The Marshall Mathers LP* this features guest appearances from fellow rappers RBX and Sticky Fingaz (of Onyx), who grab a verse each before Eminem takes over, all three coming on like zombies in a straight-to-video schlock horror movie, over a mock-spooky soundtrack cooked up by Dr Dre. RBX goes up first, all sinister and verbose, "controversial", "without no rehearsal", claiming that he'll "hit yo' ass like the train did that bitch that got Banned From TV" – a reference, this, to a supremely tasteless American television series that featured graphic, real life footage – and much loved by hip hoppers – which did indeed feature a sequence of a woman being run over by a train.

Next up is Sticky Fingaz, who nails us with his killer epigram early on – "Life's a bitch that'll fuck you if you let her" – before delivering some entertainingly psychotic bravado and earning his own alternative moniker of "Mr I-Can't-Believe-That-Nigga-Said-That".

Finally, Eminem steps to the mic and delivers a random spray of dum-dum bullets against the all usual targets – President Bill Clinton, his mother, his wife Kim ("bitch made me an angry blonde"), before a final sonic detonation from Dr Dre, as Em screams, repeatedly and worryingly into the mic, 'REMEMBER ME??," in his own mind bloodied and buried alive by his enemies but back from the dead once more.

I'M BACK

Over a slick, slowstep backbeat worked out between Em and Dre in the studio, with periodic jets of funky wah-wah, Eminem is at the top of his form here, swinging across the entire palate of his moods, from nihilistic to devilishly horny. He kicks off contemplating his miserable childhood and the fresh miseries heaped on him by fame. In a spectacularly black burst of self-pity he envies Charles Manson the security of his prison cell and laments, "What do I think of success? It sucks!" He also makes a jaundiced allusion to MTV, responsible for his commodification (their ultimate dream, a white rapper) but which would eventually distance itself from him.

In verse two, Eminem waxes sarcastic, rubbing the messy contents of his sickness in our faces, portraying himself as a corrupter of young minds, his fans like "a puppet on the string of my tennis shoe", culminating in a reference to the legs of Christopher Reeve, the actor left paralysed by a riding accident whose brave and public efforts to regain his former mobility move Slim Shady to tears of laughter.

That's as nothing compared to the next verse, however, which contains, to Eminem's chagrin, a deleted (and, it has to be said, not particularly witty) allusion to the Columbine school massacre. Eminem at least pretends to harbour a sneaking sympathy for the murderers, supposedly taking symbolic revenge on their bullying tormentors.

Much brighter and funnier are his lusty lines on Jennifer Lopez, in which he braves the potential wrath of her then-boyfriend Puff Daddy: "I'm sorry, Puff, but I don't give a fuck if this chick was my own mother/I'd still fuck her and cum inside her." Em further speculates on the confused relationship he would then have with the offspring of this imagined liaison – both a son and a new brother, though he'd disclaim responsibility for the child in any case.

In a statement, Puff Daddy generously and rather grandly waived any animosity towards Eminem for his gross impertinence. "Eminem called me and explained," he said. "We both understand this is hip hop. It's entertainment, it's not personal, so I don't have a problem with it. Every man is entitled to fantasize."

MARSHALL MATHERS

Intended, according to Eminem as a "'Just Don't Give A Fuck' Part 3", "Marshall Mathers" is the title track and the keynote one. It has what Eminem himself describes as a "front porch" feel, exacerbated by Jeff Bass's lilting vocals on the chorus and gentle acoustic strumming. You can almost imagine the crickets chirping in the background, Em out front in his vest, hacking at a twig with a penknife, ruminating on all his present hassles and bugbears, all the things that are ticking him off. However, it's barely 10 seconds before he loses it completely, stands up, hurls the knife into a tree and goes into full-on rant mode.

After an insane spiel about dragging a decapitated rottweiler around the park, shouting at it to quit barking, Em turns his attention to the late Biggie Smalls and Tupac, bitter at the inferior new wave of rappers they spawned, "cheap imitations" coining in the dollars that should have been B.I.G and Tupac's "like they switched wallets".

Fuelled up with Remy Martin, coming on like a "skinny Cartman" (the fat, obnoxious kid in South Park), he then rounds with redoubled venom on the insipid popsters still dominating the scene, from the Backstreet Boys to Ricky Martin, N'Sync to Britney ("what's this bitch, retarded? Give me back my sixteen dollars!"). There's some brilliant verbal pyrotechnics as he reminisces on a lost, golden era of gangsta, of "whylin' out and being violent", before he repays a slight delivered by Vanilla Ice to him in *Vibe*, reminding the hapless white rapper that he's just dyed his hair blonde, Eminem-style.

Vanilla gets off lightly, however, compared with Detroit horrorcore merchants Insane Clown Posse, who'd referred to "Sim Anus" on one particular track. Accusing them of ducking out of a street confrontation, Eminem unleashes the nuclear option of homophobic derision (referring to ICP's Shaggy 2 Dope and Violent J as "Faggot 2 Dope" and "Silent Gay". Those protests to MTV's Kurt Loder that Em never intended the word "faggot" as anti-gay are either forgotten or torn up as he delivers the coup de grâce: "Slim Anus? You damn right Slim Anus/I don't get fucked in mine like you two little flaming faggots!"

By now, he's utterly out of synch with Jeff Bass's acoustic accompaniment (only exploding death metal could do justice to Em's mood here), but it's all the funnier as Bass coos the chorus line, "Come and see me on the streets alone/If you assholes doubt me," as if proposing a walk around the garden.

The final verse contains another blip of self-censorship in connection with the lawsuit brought by his mother, which he refers to for the first time here, Eminem accuses the certain somebody who asserted that Em was guilty of "fabricating his past" of, shall we say, harbouring feelings of resentment towards Eminem for refusing to gratify his homosexual longings. It wouldn't be hard for anyone who had taken even just a cursory interest in the ongoing Eminem-versus-own mother legal saga to figure out who the certain somebody was. He stands by his original accusation regarding his mother, too. Where did he pick up his dope habit? "All I had to do was go in her room and lift up a mattress."

After slapping upside their heads the various people who had come out of the woodwork spuriously claiming to be relations of his since he became ultra-famous ("All of a sudden I got ninety-nine cousins!"), Eminem concludes with a vehement sneer at the magazines using his "big white ass" to sell copies before, his ill-temper finally abating, he ruefully admits, "I'll even buy a couple myself." Surely, after all, Eminem received some pleasure from becoming a pop icon?

"Marshall Mathers" is gale-force Eminem. Moreover, he would follow up some of the words here with actions. In June 2000, Em became embroiled in an argument with Douglas Dail, a member of ICP's posse, during which he allegedly brandished a firearm. The incident would hang over him for months. Meanwhile, it was the hateful words expressed here which would provide clear and stark evidence that whatever mealy-mouthed denials he might have made in the past, whatever he might claim he "really' felt on the subject, Eminem was undoubtedly guilty of expressing homophobic remarks. Organisations such as GLAAD would step up their boycotts.

DRUG BALLAD

After the full-on rage of "Marshall Mathers", "Drug Ballad" sees Eminem in a relatively cheery mood, in a verse turned round in "twenty minutes", by Em's own account. Dina Rae sweetens the deal with some funky vocal flourishes, while the Bass Brothers caper along pleasantly in the background.

This is Eminem kicking back and reminiscing about the fun time he had when he first made it big, back in the day "when Mark Wahlberg was Marky Mark," when he celebrated the first flush of euphoria by partying non-stop. Hennessy, Bacardi dark, Guinness and gin were his favoured tipples and he chuckles fondly over memories of turning into Mr Hyde (fact merges into fiction here), getting into fights, climbing in the car and driving home drunk, leaving massive pile-ups in his wake along the freeway. Whenever he makes a token effort to leave the party, he gets tugged back in by some geek – what would we have him do?

When he takes ecstasy, it tempers his normally obnoxiously confrontational nature for a while and against his better judgment he gets all lovey-dovey with a female, though he makes a swift getaway the next morning before the "bitch" can ensnare him. Eminem's clearly read the reports (conjecture, based on animal experiments, it should be pointed out) that using ecstasy might drain your spinal fluid in the long-term, but this amuses rather than frightens him. He imagines "walking around like wind dolls, shit sticking out our backs like a dinosaur."

His advice to young people is not to be deterred by scare stories, true or otherwise but to heed the call to hedonism, though you will probably end every night face down in the toilet bowl: "You're young/You've got a lot of drugs to do. Girls to screw/Parties to crash/Sucks to be you". Given his time over, Eminem vows he'd do exactly the same again, only this time in double measures. After all, he reflects, soon enough he'll be 40, nursing a bottle of Jack and two grandchildren, babysitting "While Hailie is out getting smashed!"

AMITYVILLE

Taking its name from the horror films based on the supposedly true story of a family who moved into a house in Amityville, NY, only to flee the place four weeks later after a series of hideous, paranormal events, this is Eminem's lurid take on his home town of Detroit. Eventually, at any rate. First of all, over a lurching backbeat and some low-level scratching (not that common a feature of Eminem's music), Em warms up with some nifty, almost stream-of-consciousness word play ("Pen full of ink, think sinful and rap shit"), before Bizarre, Em's compadre from D12, takes over.

Determined not to come first in any two-man Nicest Rapper competition, he delivers, in his low, deadpan tones a verse of quite stupendous obscenity, out-Emineming Eminem making even Em's normally stoical and strong-stomach record label blanch. The most appalling lines involve a brag about him inviting "10 of my boys" to deflower his little sister at a birthday party he'd arranged for her. "Guess who Slim Shady just signed to Interscope?" snickers Bizarre. This was his way of saying "Hi" to his new record company.

It's only by the third verse that Eminem gets down to the subject matter in hand, as he celebrates, with a ghoulish touch of civic pride, Detroit's status as America's number one murder capital. Why, brags Eminem, they don't do drive-by shootings in Detroit – they park up, take potshots at their victims and, when the police arrive, "shoot it out with them too!" He brandishes his own pistol by way of demonstration, as well as "a registration which made this shit valid this year." This sidelong blink at America's lax gun laws is a nice touch.

Fun as "Amityville" is, you can't help feeling Eminem's missed an opportunity here. Not necessarily for a bout of gloomy sermonizing à la Grandmaster Flash's "The Message"– that's not his style, but had he and Bizarre not spent the first couple of verses effectively fooling around, they might, between them, have riffed a bit more productively on the promising Detroit theme.

73

BITCH PLEASE II

EMINEM AT THE
POND IN ANAHEIM,
CALIFORNIA.

Featuring guest appearances from Nate Dogg, Xzibit, Snoop Dogg and Dre himself, "Bitch Please" is a public endorsement of Eminem; proof, though none were surely now needed, that he was considered a fully-fledged member of the rap fraternity. Over a classy, silvery backbeat, they take turns on the mic, Dre in his usual ill-tempered persona, Xzibit gangsta to the hilt ("I might leave in the bodybag but never in cuffs"). Snoop's style, as ever, is slinkier and wilier, as he introduces Eminem as his "nephew" and "the Great White American Hope", making light and play of issues such as ethnicity and authenticity, which for many critics are dense and vexed ones.

Eminem repays the homage with a brilliant impersonation of "Uncle" Snoop's languid, Southern twang, before calling out Timothy White, the man who had condemned him in *Billboard* magazine for "making a living off the world's misery", a sentence recycled here by Eminem. Bantering with his intellectual foes, rapping round the theme of the malicious intentions in his lyrics, Em leaves the issue nicely unresolved: "Somewhere deep down, there's a decent human being in me. It just can't be found." Or certainly has no wish to put itself out front in his songs, at any rate.

KIM

Among Eminem's critics, this is one of his most reviled numbers, culminating, as it does, in a dramatized enactment of him murdering his wife Kim and screaming "Bleed, bitch, bleed!" as she chokes to death. These lines are mentioned in practically every profile of Eminem, especially those wishing to highlight what they see as his worst excesses. For example at salon.com Eric Boehlert wondered why his fellow critics were so indulgent of Eminem and gave even abominable lyrics like this "a pass". Eminem himself unrepentantly and theatrically highlighted the song live, taking a blow-up doll onstage and stabbing at it with a dagger while performing "Kim".

"Kim" can't be explained or excused as cartoon violence or satire. It isn't either. It's a perturbingly heartfelt song, written at a time when Eminem was again estranged from his wife. He said himself he had intended to sit down and write a love song but didn't want to resort to the usual cooey blandishments, instead writing something that expressed his inner feelings – "I wanted to scream." The result is a repugnant, yet blood-raw and gripping performance, draining for all concerned. And, despite Boelhert and co's misgivings, it deserves not just a pass but a distinction. At the very least it deserves to be listened to properly and in context.

Working over a heavy, turbulent backbeat concocted by the Bass Brothers, reminiscent of John Bonham's concussive playing on Led Zeppelin's "When The Levee Breaks", "Kim" begins softly with Eminem locked in solicitous babytalk with his daughter Hailie, before rounding suddenly on his wife: "You move again, I'll beat the shit out of you!"

This isn't the usual, casual hip hop misogynistic, between-the-boys banter. What we've stumbled horribly onto is a very, very bad domestic row. By Em's account, Kim has cheated on him. Whether she did or not, either in the context of the song or in real life, hardly matters. It's the hoarse, crazed emotions of a man twisting on the edge of his tether than count here – and Eminem's unflinching depiction of them. He plays the part of Kim, too, shrieking and pleading for her life. Tellingly, Em refrains from the usual prissy-wissy tones he normally adopts when impersonating the opposite sex. He at least does Kim the justice of conveying her abject terror.

Only the chorus lets the song down a little, with Eminem attempting to sing, loudly and flatly: "Bitch you did me so wrong/I don't want to go on." The real red meat is in the verses, with Eminem clearly as much tormented as tormentor, confused and crumbling inside: "I swear to God I hate you!/

Oh my God, I love you!"… Oh my God, I'm cracking up…" a lyrical moment where he breaks off to give vent to a bout of road rage as they swerve along the highway. At times he's pathetic, cripplingly insecure: "Why don't you like me?/You think I'm ugly, don't you?"

By the final verse, however, he's stone cold and bent on his terrible, final deed. He's already killed Kim's lover and her four-year-old boy, now he's calculating how to make the whole thing look like a double homicide and suicide on Kim's part, cackling dementedly, beyond hope.

Although "Kim" is pure fantasy, it's authentic in that it's precisely the sort of fantasy in which Eminem might have indulged in his darkest, most furious moments, estranged from his wife and kid. It's a superbly detailed revisitating of those feelings (Em claimed to have written it while on mood-amplifying E), a great piece of musical drama which, although highly subjective, is rounded enough for us to come to our own judgments. However, it ended up being dropped from the "clean" version of the album. Only Eminem could have recorded a song like "Kim", working through the blunt and prosaic form of rap but able to lay bare his open emotional wounds in a way usually unheard of in hip hop. Its awfulness is a thing of awe. When he sat Kim down and played it to her, when they were reconciled, he told her, "I know this is a fucked-up song but it shows how much I care about you. To even think about you this much. To put you on a song like this." Again, Kim was reluctant to buy the argument that this was the sort of "care" she needed. "You're fucking crazy," she told him. One can only be grateful that Eminem at least vented his anger through this sort of "therapy" and not through actual violence. Later, however, after seeing footage of Em kicking a doll-likeness of her around on stage, Kim slit her wrists. If "Kim" was art or a test of the legitimacy of self-expression, it came at a perilously high price.

UNDER THE INFLUENCE

After "Kim", a slight breather and a bit of a singalong with the boys from D12. Eminem opens proceedings with an unapologetically slack chorus: "I was high when I wrote this so suck my dick." Then the D12 posse – Swifty, Bizarre, Proof, Kuniva and Kon Artis – follow up to the mic. Anyone expecting them to divulge their Zodiac signs will be disappointed. Between them, D12 muster a few very good lines. "Even on the Million Man March, we're gonna fight," says Swifty, while Bizarre talks about having to give his pitbull an abortion after having sex with it while out of it on cocaine.

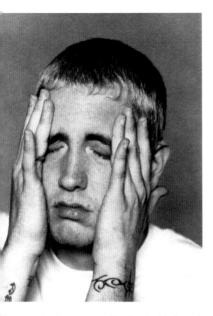

Maybe Eminem trumps them all, however, taking the rap biscuit for originality by describing himself as "like a wasp in the hospital/Lost, stinging the fuck outta everything." It's the "lost" that clinches it. Once again, you have to ask yourself, where did he pull that one from?

CRIMINAL

And so, with all the pomp and ceremony of a priest making his final address at a church service, against the ecclesiastic drones of a distant organ, Eminem has his final word. Once again, he wearily takes to task those out there dumb enough to believe he actually believes all the things that he says on his records and once again, he yanks their tails. "'Cause I'm a CRIMINAL!" he declares, over a looping piano riff and he's off,

EMINEM'S RISE TO INTERNATIONAL STARDOM DID NOT COME WITHOUT AN EMOTIONAL COST.

flipping the bird one last time, Slim Shady-style. "Criminal" is intended by Eminem as another defiant snook in the "Don't Give A Fuck" mode. "It's the last song on the record," he said. "It sums up the whole album."

He taunts the gay rights lobby for starters, disinterring the corpse of the fashion designer Versace, murdered in 1997 outside his house by serial killer Andrew Cunanan, for a cheap laugh. "Whoops, somebody shot me! And I was checking the mail!/Get it? Checking the 'male'." Proof, this, that while the devil may have all the best tunes, he also has some of the worst jokes.

Thereafter, he cavorts about like the kid who refuses to take his medication and disrupts the rest of the class. "You can't teach me a goddamn thing, 'cause/I watch TV and Comcast cable/And you ain't able to stop these thoughts." If he's bad, it's because every moral authority in his life, from televangelists secretly on the make, to a President having oral sex in the White House, meant that "his morals went thhhbbppp." Then there was his own mother. As he puts it with brilliant succinctness here, "How you s'posed to grow up when you weren't raised?"

But it's impossible for anyone to take Slim's schtick seriously even if they want to. When he talks about blasting away Dr Dre with an AK, you hardly imagine the producer quaking in his boots, while lines like "This puppy's lucky I didn't blast his ass yet" tend to undermine the menace of the song. As Eminem guessed, in case no one had figured it out, "Half the shit I say, I just make up/To make you mad."

"Criminal" is punctuated by a skittish interlude in which he delivers a cameo as a trigger-happy bank robber, oblivious to his getaway driver's pleas not to shoot the teller. This routine took much of a studio day to get right, not least because Mel-Man, playing the driver, was drunk and kept forgetting his lines.

THE KIDS

When Em's record company decided to issue a separate, "clean" version of *The Marshall Mathers LP*, minus the controversial "Kim", they needed a track to draft in its place. Whereupon Eminem came up with the thoroughly wholesome and suitable "The Kids", in which Slim Shady is drafted in as a substitute teacher at South Park Elementary to deliver a lecture about the evils of drugs. Eminem gets to do his very funny, very accurate impressions of both Mr Mackey, the counsellor at South Park Elementary, and Cartman, the fat kid with the fast mouth, whom Eminem often compared himself to, both in song and interview. His Cartman interventions are especially comic – it's not that often we get to hear the fat boy in full-on expletive mode. ("Suck my motherfuckin' penis!").

"The Kids" sees Slim Shady deliver three ridiculous anti-drugs homilies, each a satire on the moral panic and misinformation surrounding the drugs debate in America, marked by the dark, descending chords that make up the musical backdrop. In the first, "Bob", a pot smoker who lives with his mom, murders and dismembers a local waitress – a classic example, tuts Slim, of what marijuana can do to you. Now meet Zach, an ecstasy user who experiences instant loss of spinal fluid (an alleged symptom of excessive E use already noted by Em on "Drugs Ballad") leaving his back deformed, looking like "the MacDonald's arches". Finally, we address one of the most dangerous drugs of all, "fungus" (magic mushrooms) which, given that it grows in fields, amid cow manure, is not only apt to give you hallucinations but also to make your tongue swell up, just like a cow's.

In between all this comes the chorus, led by Mr Mackey in his gormless, midwestern drawl, telling us that "drugs are baad" and urging kids to "Say no to drugs/So you don't act like everyone else does." Finally, as Kenny, the regularly ill-fated kid in the duffel coat dies of a mushroom overdose ("Oh, my God!"), Slim reveals his real reasons for urging drugs abstinence – "So there'll be more for me!"

Underpinning all of this is Eminem's conviction that, regardless of whether he were to implore kids to do drugs or implore them not to, his words would have zero impact. Kids would carry on as ever doing drugs, as would many of their parents.

BAD INFLUENCE

Not included on this album, "Bad Influence" is the B-side to "The Way I Am", which would be included on the soundtrack to *End Of Days*, delivered over crashing waves of hip hop rhythm that anticipate the heavier vibe of *The Eminem Show*.

The opening gambit of this song is all that remains from a ream of scribbled thoughts which Eminem then mislaid, as the bit of paper went missing from his California apartment. In it Em counters the accusation that he's a bad influence by stating, half-seriously, "I say the world's fucked, I'm just adding to it."

And now he's off to the races, galloping past Lauryn Hill, Brandy and Mase, flicking each in the face with his lyrical whip, rounding a now-familiar and well-beaten circuit of preoccupations, including his shitty childhood, his mock-suicidal tendencies and his refusal to accept the invidious mantle of role model. Things do perk up in the final lines as he namechecks Gilbert's Lodge, where he used to work in a menial capacity while struggling to launch his career, breaking off to chide his fans for not picking up on him sooner.

Finally, he responds to the antipathy generated by his treatment of Kim on "Just The Two Of Us" and, knowingly goading those who think of him as a "chauvinist pig", reveals that, in spite of everything, they've reconciled: "The funny shit is I still go with the bitch." A triumphant slap to his detractors but, for all the self-justification intended here, did Eminem really think his relationship could survive this sort of knockabout lyrical abuse?

D12 DEVIL'S NIGHT

"There was like a personal agreement we made when we first got together years ago in Detroit," said Eminem of D12, also known as the Dirty Dozen for reasons that become instantly obvious on listening to their product. "If any of us made it, we'd bring the others along and do something together."

In 2001, Eminem was true to his word when he put his own career on hold to cut the Shady Records' album *Devil's Night* with his old posse, whose original idea had been, in the words of founder member Proof, to "bring the freshest, best MCs in Detroit together in one group, a supergroup thing."

Proof, aka Dirty Harry (real name DeShaun Holton) had formed D12 back in 1990 when he was in his mid-teens. He would eventually be joined by Bizarre, aka Peter S, (Rufus Johnson), Kon Artis, aka Mr Denine Porter (Denaun Porter), Kuniva, aka Rondell Beane (Von Carlisle) and Bugz, aka Robert Beck (Cornell Pitts), who was murdered in 1999 following an altercation at a party, and to whom *The Marshall Mathers LP* was co-dedicated. Bugz was replaced by Swifty, aka Swifty McVay (Ondre Moore). Eminem himself had known Proof since he was 15 and the pair of them would compete on the mic at the Hip hop Shop on Detroit's 7 Mile, experiences which would form the basis for the rap battles in the film *8 Mile*. "As soon as I got on the mic, I'd get booed," recalled Eminem. "Once the motherfuckers heard me rhyme, though, they shut up."

It was while looking for beats for his debut album *Infinite* that Eminem consolidated his links with D12, using Kon Artis on the album and, through him, meeting Bizarre. The concept of D12 was hatched by Proof on a car journey from New York, in which he devised the idea of the Dirty Dozen – six members plus their alter egos making up the complement of 12. It was round about this time that Eminem had had his epiphany while astride the toilet and Slim Shady was born – he was among the last of D12 to devise an alter ego.

D12 first recorded together on *The Underground EP*, a hard-to-find item that received a limited release in 1997. Eminem features on three of the tracks but he's in no way distinguishable from the rest of his crew except by his skin colour – there are certainly none of the graphic, autobiographical concerns of his best work. On "Chance To Advance" he talks of running over "bitches", leaving them flat "like bar codes" in the road. On "Filthy" he talks himself up as a "rap pervert", serving "dirt" but not really delivering. On "Bring Our Boys" awkward lines like "I guard my sector like a St Bernard" suggest a latent talent still in its green stages.

The next time D12 appeared together was on "Under The Influence" on *The Marshall Mathers LP.* The various solo members had had limited success under their individual monikers – Bizarre's 1997 EP *Attack Of The Weirdos*, for instance. It wasn't until 2001, however, that D12 enjoyed huge success under their own name, their prospects undoubtedly boosted massively by Eminem's immense commercial cachet. "No one in this group is above anyone else,not even Eminem" says Kuniva, adding realistically "…it's just that he's sold a lot of albums. And we haven't sold shit yet!"

Devil's Night, preceded by the single "Shit On You", ascended instantaneously to the top of both the US and UK albums charts on its release in June 2001. Kuniva had warned readers of The Source what to expect: "Get ready for the sickness," he had advised them. The opening "Public Service Announcement" also gave fair warning. Anybody, it said, who objected to terms like "lesbian", "faggot" and "fudgepacker" should

turn off now. Bizarre, in particular, revels in soiling his raps with imagery so appalling, so beyond the pale that it's actually impossible to try to condemn it's deleterious impact on America's youth while keeping a straight face.

The album received mixed reviews, with some writers feeling that the D12 posse brought out the boorish worst in each other, as they seemed to attempt to out-gross each other on the mic. Certainly, listening to *Devil's Night*, you can't help but feel it was no accident of fate that Eminem was the one that finally made it out of D12. His contributions, on which this chapter will primarily concentrate, are the album's strongest and most distinctive features, even if he is holding back his absolute top-drawer stuff. Still, D12 are no mean rappers, and all of them have their moments, particularly the often magnificently disgusting Bizarre.

Watching the CD-Rom documentary that accompanies the special edition of this album, you realize that these boys keep a suitably ironic and mirthful distance from their subject matter. Moreover, it's interesting to note that in the sleevenotes, the D12 boys (with the exception of Eminem himself) belie their demonic and misogynist posturings, offering sweetly profuse gratitude to the ladies in their lives, including their moms, and pious thanks to "God the creator" for his part in bringing to us the deranged, often inspired, filth of *Devil's Night*.

EMINEM 'CAME BACK FOR HIS OLD DETROIT POSSE, ONCE HE HAD FOUND FAME.

Eminem appears on all the tracks on *Devil's Night* bar the following: "Nasty Mind", a Dre-produced, determinedly evil farrago of gang-banging braggadocio on which Bizarre dreams of "fucking a handicapped bitch"; "That's How", an intricately ordered piece of ensemble rapping which quotes from Curtis Mayfield's "(Don't Worry) If There's Hell Below We're All Gonna Go", in which the boys reminisce mockingly on Em's volatile relationship with Kim; "Instigator", on which Swifty, Kuniva and Kon Artis boast about deliberately stirring up street trouble just for the hell of it as rotor blades whirl overhead; and "Obie Trice", on which Eminem's rap protege of the same name makes a guest appearance.

SHIT CAN HAPPEN

The jaunty beat and squiggly electronics of this opener offer a musical hint that D12 are playing with us here, having fun trying to make us blanch at their revolting lyrical antics, even as Kuniva warns, "This ain't funny so don't you dare laugh," in case we don't take their threats of leaving us in need of paramedics altogether seriously.

It's only when the baton is passed to Eminem that the track really jump-starts. Armed to the lyrical teeth, "Young and ornery, worse than my Uncle Ronnie", he's all twitchy and itching for some foolhardy MC or pop celeb to bad-mouth him so that he can let loose on them. "When I'm bent, most of my energy is spent on enemies," he spits, and most of that energy is alcohol-fuelled, from "Hennessy, preferred gangsta tipple". Finally, he issues what amounts to the D12 manifesto: "Insanity spills from the mentality of twelve motherfuckers/In six different bodies with their personalities split." Once again he warns us that "this is not a motherfucking joke."

But then, he would say that. Such are the conveniences of a split personality.

PISTOL PISTOL

Squeamishly asterisked out on the cover sleeve track listing, "Pistol Pistol" totes an already-familiar theme of homicidal menace to the morbid accompaniment of what could be the soundtrack to a straight-to-video horror B-movie. In mock-violation of his parole conditions, Eminem informs us, and the police officer in the lyric who confronts him, that he goes nowhere without his gun.

But it's Bizarre who takes the honours here, ranting about the mystical powers of his firearm, whose persuasive powers are such that it will "make Christopher Reeve start walking" (the disabled former star of the Superman movies is a perennial object of Eminem and D12's lurid fascination), make a Muslim dye his hair blonde, turn a nun into a "filthy slut" and, finally, make Slim Shady fall back in love with Christina Aguilera.

AIN'T NUTTIN' BUT MUSIC

Featuring Dre Dre, whose artificial synth backdrop is part lampoon of the fake plastic pop Eminem despises, part play for the same market, "Ain't Nuttin' But Music" is primarily a showcase for Eminem to make another dirty play for Britney Spears, despite their musical differences. He's at a loss here to understand why she can lavish her favours on Ben Affleck but not him. "Goddamn it, I'm rich, bitch," he pleads, though he's not exactly down on one knee. Wistfully, he reflects that the closest he is ever likely to get to Britney sexually, or to "hitting it from the back," is on the doctored pictures of the two of them on the Internet.

Which anal activity reminds him of his latest feud, this time with House of Pain's Everlast and DJ Lethal of Limp Bizkit, both of whom dissed him and whom, it follows, according to the logic of gangsta grievance, are both enthusiastically homosexual.

In the chorus, however, Eminem switches tone as he and Dre intone, "What's going on in the world today/People fighting, feuding, looting, it's OK/Let it go, let it flow, let the good times roll/Tell 'em Dre (it ain't nuttin' but music)." As *Rolling Stone* reviewer Nathan Brackett put it, this is, "A reminder that we live in a world where rap-lyric controversies get as much press as, say, race riots in Cincinnati." It's a reminder also that Eminem is able to slip out

of his nasty personae, slip off his high horse at will and shed a beam of sanity on the panic and nonsense generated around him by the media.

AMERICAN PSYCHO

Taking its title from the Brett Easton Ellis novel, Eminem delivers another twisted and grotesquely comical homage to his own depravity. "I'm a devil ... a human mutt," he leers, over an eerie, pattering backbeat which sounds like mysterious footsteps in the night. He even hints that he may be aware of the Viz character Buster Gonad and his unfeasibly large testicles as he boasts that,

LEFT: D12'S KUNIVA
IN CONCERT,
LONDON 2001
RIGHT: BIZARRE -
THE POSSE'S MOST
OUTRAGEOUS
LYRICIST.

so big are his own gonads that he might as well "Unzip my fly and let 'em fall to the floor." More likely, this is a case of great and foul minds thinking alike.

So warped are his thoughts that he begins speaking in tongues at one point, before another demonstration of his multisyllabic proficiency and impatience with the limits of language as he goes into phonetic overdrive: "Just goes to shizzow you dizzon't, fizzuck with so-someone this disturbed, sa-sipping on sizurp…"

PURPLE PILLS

The most notorious track to be culled from D12, this brazen paean to the joys of taking coke and in particular ecstasy had to be re-christened with the frankly nonsensical title "Purple Hills" before it was deemed eligible for airplay.

To the toxic soundtrack of a tipsy-sounding saxophone and the mischievous chatter of munchkins (or is it attacks of the munchies?), Eminem takes us on what can only be called a grand tour of narcotics and hallucinogens, including uppers, downers and a trip up and down "mushroom mountain".

He somehow manages to squeeze in yet another tasteless allusion to the disabled Superman actor Christopher Reeve, followed by a brilliant slap to Vanilla Ice, who had, in the wake up Eminem's success, decided that the time was coincidentally ripe to resuscitate his own career. "I see dumb shit happening/Dumber than Vanilla Ice trying to rap again," snickers Em, before alerting Bizarre to his mom, passed out on the couch.

On the chorus, the entire posse pretends to be so out of it on whatever that they practically nod out in mid-line, babbling comatosely.

Not surprisingly, none of this remotely amused Janet Betts, the mother of Leah Betts, the teenager whose death from ecstasy made her the most high-profile British casualty of the drug, and which triggered what some would describe as a media-driven moral panic concerning E.

She urged broadcasters everywhere to boycott "Purple Hills", stating in *The Sun* newspaper that Eminem was "…an icon to teenagers. They will hear this and think it's cool to take drugs."

FIGHT MUSIC

A sort of rap corollary to the film *Fight Club*, "Fight Music" features the distant background noise of lairy male yelping, a tortuous metal guitar riff and some choppy string bass, as Eminem comes out swinging punches in a pre-emptive assault on his critics. "It's just some shit, for these kids to trash their rooms with," he asserts, at once playing up his music as an escape valve for adolescent frustration and playing it down as being nothing more serious or harmful than that.

After verses from his D12 comrades, during which Bizarre once again takes the biscuit with a line about oral sex with his grandmother, Em's built up a head of steam and is giddy with over-the-top evangelical zeal. He rails against a confederation that's formed against him in his own mind of "racists and hypocrites… Liberaces, Versaces and Nazis," by which he means those who would fascistically infringe on his freedom of speech by slamming his anti-gay lyrics. Lapsing into self-righteousness as is (very) occasionally his wont, Eminem talks himself up as the saviour of an entire generation whose parents "failed to raise 'em 'cause they're lazy" and, again not quite joining the logical dots together, ends by dedicating the song to "any kid who gets picked on". This was always Eminem's defence when he was accused, by gay rights activists for instance, of providing grist to the mill of bullying gay-bashers – that he knew as well as anybody what it was like to be bullied and that the pugnacity in his music was that of a worm turning.

EMINEM WITH
PROOF, A FRIEND
FROM HIS TEENAGE
YEARS.

PIMP LIKE ME

Typically grotesque, bitch-slapping fare this, with Eminem's sole contribution
coming on the chorus with longtime female collaborator Dina Rae. As Em
jeers, "You just a…", "You're just my…" and "Dirty ass", Rae finishes his
sentences with a soulful cry of "ho", cooing assent as he growls "I'm yo'
pimp, you my bitch."

But Ms Rae is no traitor to her gender, nor singing under sufferance. As
a choreographer and singer in her own right, there was no shortage of
respect for Dina Rae from Eminem and his production team, who have
praised her ability to improvise the sort of melodic lines which have
sweetened numerous Eminem cuts.

Some might prefer it if Dina Rae came back with some sassy, hands-on-
hips, hush-yo' mouth comebacks when Em starts cheeking her, but that
would be comedically lame, puncturing the Slim Shady persona for the sake
of political correctness. It'd be going too far to say that the mutual respect

between Rae and Eminem is glaringly obvious from this track but mutual respect there is. Dina Rae gave to *Vibe* magazine her own fond, and probably accurate character assessment of Eminem, the man who had consistently helped put her voice out front in the R&B world: "Sweet. Sensitive. Shy".

BLOW MY BUZZ

More sleazy, Bacchalanian P-Funk, (or is it G-Funk?) in which Eminem points up the dangers of drugs misuse, not so much as a finger-wagging warning to kids but almost as a gauntlet. Unless, he asserts, you exhibit various symptoms, including a tendency to psychosis, your "tongue rotting out from cotton-mouth", a case of the munchies so severe that you "end up spending a G in the vending machine" and extreme paranoia, then frankly, you're a bit of a drugs cissy. In real life, Eminem's drugs use has probably been a good deal more moderate than he alleges in his lyrics – if you're to believe his interviews during his period on probation, anyhow.

EMINEM AND BIZARRE RAP AT THE LEEDS FESTIVAL, ENGLAND 2001.

DEVIL'S NIGHT

The name of the title track of the album is taken from an annual Detroit pastime, in which, on the night before Halloween, local hoodlums would traditionally run amok, burning derelict houses to the ground, as seen in the film *8 Mile*. Here, Eminem facetiously puts the willies up his more highly-strung critics, taunting them with all their worst fears about his music. He plays himself up as a rap Dracula who makes "hate music like devil worshipping Satan music" in the face of which even makeshift crucifixes are futile.

He namechecks Kurt Cobain, whom many saw as Eminem's closest musical cousin in recent years, with the pair as two trash blondes making huge artistic capital out of their private angst. He sweepingly and sarcastically refers to the generations of kids who blew their brains out to his music or went out and "murdered and maimed to it", like psychotic lemmings open to every suggestion made in rock or rap. It's another devastating riposte to those panicky right-wingers who blame music for all America's ills, as if the country was in a state of rude moral health until heavy metal and hip hop came along.

REVELATION

The chorus here is reminiscent of Pink Floyd's "Another Brick In The Wall" ("I don't need no education"), a comparison boosted by what sounds like a parody of Dave Gilmour's guitar solo on that single, the culmination of a suitably Gothic and strung-out backbeat. With amoral fervour, D12 espouse their nihilistic creed in the chorus – forget saving the world, forget making anything of yourself because you're not long for this world in any case.

After the portly Bizarre once more slanders his poor dear grandmother ("the bitch got AIDS"), Eminem weighs in with a verse in which he extols the all-American creed of self-help and hard work. He was failed, he says, by the educational system but redeemed by hip hop, a university from which he graduated with honours. He goes on to deplore those who had it easy, but who nonetheless don't share his work ethic: "A fucking drop-out that quits/Stupid as shit, rich as fuck and proud of it."

Once again, the more Eminem warms to a theme, the more the Shady mask slips and the more he surprises you when he reveals some of his core, sometimes conservative, values.

GIRLS

This bonus track is a chance for Eminem to (over) extend himself on the subject of his aforementioned grudge against DJ Lethal of Limp Bizkit, Everlast and, by extension, Bizkit's Fred Durst. Everlast and Eminem had had a beef that dated back to the former House Of Pain rapper's taking a shot at Eminem when he guested on "The Dilated Peoples' Ear Drums Pop". Eminem retorted with "I Remember", which appeared as the B-side to "Shit On You", and they'd been feuding ever since.

DJ Lethal was caught in the middle of the crossfire here, having been in House of Pain with Everlast himself but also being friends with Eminem. He'd initially said that the pair would sort out their differences "like men" but, when forced to choose who would prevail in an ass-whipping contest between the pair, plumped for Everlast.

DJ Lethal also backed out of appearing on "Quitter", a track on which he'd been due to guest, which called for all right-thinking fans to physically attack Everlast. Eminem felt a deep sense of betrayal, by Bizkit frontman Fred Durst also, as both had been friends. This accounts for what is an overlong and over-indulgent rant.

Had he left it at the first verse it would have been OK, culminating as it does in Eminem at his best – raw, direct, enraged, seeming to leap right off the deck and grab you by the throat.

But then there's two more verses of it, in which he comes on more and more like a pub bore, going round in ever-increasing circles of ineffectual doggerel. All that redeems this exercise is a fleeting allusion to how he would "fight for Kim", taken by some as a small note of atonement for his past lyrical antipathy towards her – though small is certainly the word.

SHIT ON YOU

The first single to be issued prior to the release of the D12 album, "Shit On You" is musically nimble, the beat tiptoeing discreetly in the background, but lyrically less so. The chorus is Eminem's, his excremental threat issued to all-comers. And, he reveals, if indeed it comes as any surprise, that he thrives on the various beefs and feuds he is perpetually fighting on so many fronts: "…How boring it gets/When there's no one to hit."

He knows he's hypersensitive to disses and perceived disses – "Over reaction is my only reaction" – which itself sets off a "chain reaction" mimicked in the dazzling, zig-zagging switchblade wordplay that follows: "More zaniac than maniacs in action/A rat pack in black jackets who pack ten…" (The first two lines here were lifted from the title track of his debut *Infinite*, the one track he was still proud of on that album.) Once again, however, Eminem is at his sharpest and most epigrammatic when brooding on what should have been his formative years: "I never grew up, I was born grown and grew down."

WORDS ARE WEAPONS

On this bonus track, available on the European bonus disc, Eminem seems to be suffering from a feeling of firearm withdrawal, following his conviction for weapons possession. "Those cock-sucking cops got my Smith-N-Wesson," he grumbles. Fortunately, as the title affirms, his words are his real weapons, which he uses to "crush my opponents." Still, that's no consolation for being deprived of the ability to grab onto something long and hard in your pocket. The feeling of emasculation at this "confiscation" probably accounts for the almost hysterical pitch of vocal frenzy Em reaches here, breaching the conventions of hip hop cool by raising his voice: "They jealous of you man, that's the only reason they beefin'!"

THESE DRUGS

Another track available only on the European bonus disc, in "These Drugs" Eminem squanders his verse, re-roasting old chestnuts about the effect of his music on his fans. More entertaining are his spoken word narratives, delivered over the top of the chorus, to the accompaniment of a hazy, loping, psychedelic guitar loop. In the first, he talks about passing out following a surfeit of coke; in the second describes how he was completely out of it every night on his first tour; while in the third he speculates prosaically, almost matter-of-factly, that drugs will one day be his undoing, that we'll one day soon pick up a paper headlining with his death of an overdose. "It's just peer pressure," he shrugs, though you suspect more than a pinch of self-dramatisation here.

THE EMINEM SHOW

The 20 months between *The Marshall Mathers LP* and The Eminem Show were loaded with incident, controversy, fresh antagonism and familial breakdown, all of which provided grief and grist alike for Eminem, now on the point of becoming probably the biggest, and certainly the most notorious, recording artist in the world. He would be both feted and reviled by senior members of the pop aristocracy, while both church and state would begin to pay serious heed to the angry blonde, the saviour and devil who was becoming synonymous for many with the volatile, restless state of American youth.

In June 2000, still smarting over the feud with Insane Clown Posse, Eminem became involved in an altercation with Douglas Dail, one of their entourage, outside a stereo shop in Royal Oak, Michigan, during which he allegedly produced a semi-automatic firearm. Kim, with him at the time, sailed loyally into the fray and into the face of Dail's wife. The police arrived and Eminem admitted to carrying a concealed weapon.

That, however, wasn't the end of it. That same weekend, Eminem was again arrested, this time outside the Hot Rocks cafe club in Warren, Michigan. He'd driven out there convinced that his wife was seeing another man. On arriving at the scene, he was incensed to spot Kim kissing another man, one John Guerra, in the car park. Again, he was alleged to have produced a handgun which he brandished and with which he was accused of hitting Guerra in the head and face, as well as threatening to kill him. Guerra conceded that the kiss he had received from Kim was "rather intimate" but, having been scared out of his wits by the rather less affectionate attentions of her husband, he filed a civil suit against the rapper.

Again, Kim became involved, this time the worse for drink and, in her excitement and hysteria, landed herself with charges of misdemeanour and disturbing the peace. (She would later get off with a $50 fine and an order to attend an Alcoholics Anonymous meeting).

The two incidents, following as they did so quickly on each other, could have had grave consequences for Eminem. Now facing a charge of assault as well as one of carrying an unlicensed concealed weapon, he was looking at the possibility, if not the likelihood, of a lengthy jail sentence. Speaking to *The Face*, he put out a front of macho defiance, stating that, "Whatever happens happens… being thrown in jail, none of that shit bothers me."

Still worse, however, the incident in Warren meant that his on-off relationship with Kim was off again. They continued to share the same house but after he filed for divorce in July, she sued him for $10 million, citing the emotional distress caused by Em, not least in his murdering an effigy of her onstage. Mathers' lawyer in her misdemeanour case remarked of her passivity in the face of songs like "Kim" and "'97 Bonnie & Clyde", "I don't know any other person on the planet who could endure what she did." Indeed, that same July she had attempted suicide, attempting to slit her wrists at the Detroit home she still shared with her husband.

Eventually, however, the divorce went through, in October 2001, though not before Kim had dropped her lawsuit against Em and the couple had even reconciled briefly one last time, before papers were again issued the following March.

In the meantime, Eminem was showered with both awards and invective from the gay and lesbian lobby. He was also attacked on the floor of the US Senate by Lynne Cheney, wife of future Vice President Dick Cheney. She expressed her disgust at a music industry which could honour a man

93

responsible for such "despicable material". Yet during this time, Eminem found himself with a new and unlikely friend and ally – Elton John, who had expressed his admiration for Eminem and, to the further disgust of Mrs Cheney, agreed to duet with him at the Grammy Awards in February 2001, performing a version of "Stan" (with Elton replacing Dido). Though it was only very recent news to Eminem that Elton John was gay, he was only too grateful for his endorsement and he intended the Grammys' duet as a rebuke against those who accused him of homophobia. "People take my shit out of context," he protested. But his detractors remained unimpressed and Eminem faced further demonstrations and a chorus of disapproval, on both sides of the Atlantic. Peter Tatchell, the UK Gay Rights activist, stated that Eminem's nomination for a Brit Award was "the moral equivalent of honouring a Ku Klux Klan singer".

The pop world was divided over Eminem. Sheryl Crow said, "To be perfectly, honest, [Eminem] is not apologising for what he says about gays and [I think that] people side with him because he's cool and cutting edge… but I don't agree with them at all."

Moby, meanwhile, who had recently been launched to unlikely superstar status relatively late in his career with his album *Play*, was forthright in his anti-Eminem stance, which would lead to a lengthy feud between the pair. Speaking to the NME, he conceded that while Eminem "is very good at what he does," he found some of his songs to be "unbelievably offensive. Especially considering the people who are buying his records are nine and 10-year-olds and his songs are about misogyny, homophobia, rape and

LYNNE CHENEY CONDEMNED EMINEM AS A "VIOLENT MISOGYNIST".

abuse. I'm 35. I can understand the ambiguity and the irony. Nine and 10-year-olds cannot."

And yet, when their views were canvassed by the *LA Times*, a number of pop superstars rallied to Eminem. Madonna stated that she found the language of President George W Bush "much more offensive" than anything uttered by Eminem. "He's making people's blood boil, he's reflecting what's going on in society right now," she said. Elton John reiterated his pro-Eminem stance, praising the rapper's "black sense of humour". And in response to songwriter Jimmy Webb's assertion that to award Eminem a Grammy would damage the ceremony's "moral credibility", Stevie Wonder remarked that, "There was a time when the blues were considered a disgrace."

As he hit the road for a European tour, Eminem found himself a magnet for controversy and censure, with sundry religious groups and figures cottoning on to the trick of drawing attention to themselves by drawing attention to Eminem's iniquities. In Italy, the Archbishop of Turin echoed the sentiments of Cardinal Poletto, who, deploring TV station RAI's support for Eminem, declared, "We have to help young people decide between good and bad."

MADONNA
RETORTED THAT SHE
FOUND CHENEY'S
HUSBAND'S BOSS,
GEORGE W BUSH,
MORE OFFENSIVE.

A Scottish religious group, the Catholic Charismatic Renewal Group, would later attempt to block both Eminem and his buddy Marilyn Manson from playing the Gig On The Green festival. It blamed Eminem for "our youngsters [becoming] more rebellious and aggressive", and suggested that Marilyn Manson was "a committed member of the Church of Satan".

It was in the swirl of all this, plus the litigious attentions of his mother still flapping overhead, that Eminem wrote, recorded and released *The Eminem Show*. The title reflected the ambivalence with which Em greeted his swelling fame and notoriety. Part of him resented the fact that his life had been turned into a public spectacle. Having ill-advisedly bought a house in Detroit quite close to a public highway, he found himself plagued by fans and "well-wishers", who lobbed empty packs of M&Ms over the fence. He would subsequently move out to an exclusive, gated property, images of which are plastered all over the cover art of *The Eminem Show*, coupled with CCTV cameras – an obvious allusion to celebrity surveillance, though it was Em, as fascinated as anyone by his own fame, who was training the cameras on himself.

Yet another part of him relished the limelight, the bouquets and brickbats, the nonsense . "We need a little controversy/'Cause it feels so empty without me," he sneered, with the barbed arrogance of a latterday hip hop Johnny Rotten, on "Without Me", the single which preceded *The Eminem Show*. He also paid tribute to his fans, who appear in their multitudes in the videos for the singles taken from the album, especially "Sing For The Moment". He enthused on "White America" about the feeling of "having an army marching in back of me." Modern music, right now, was indeed *The Eminem Show*. He was the star, and almost the only attraction in a scene rendered anaemic by instant pop, rendered anonymous by techno and electronica, in which rock was becoming increasingly bloated and fossilized, fit only for the VH-1 museum or its own hall of fame.

ON STAGE FOR THE 45TH ANNUAL GRAMMY AWARDS AT MADISON SQUARE GARDEN IN 2003.

Only hip hop still bristled with life and Eminem was not only hip hop's biggest star, he had transcended the genre (although hip hop itself had also accelerated past the medium-paced Dre-beats Eminem still kept faith with). On *The Eminem Show*, Em would take on a bigger, rockier dimension, rock having long since been annexed by hip hop with Run-DMC/Aerosmith's "Walk This Way". No longer a novice in the studio, he knew what he wanted, knew what he was doing. "Now I know how I want my shit to sound," he said. "We treated this record like it was a rock record." These were Eminem's new territories. Now, he was king of the world, a weighty pop-cultural proposition assuming a suitably weighty sound.

The Eminem Show was the biggest selling album of 2002, selling over 8 million copies. He followed up with an Anger Management tour, in which songs like "White America" and "My Dad's Gone Crazy" were accompanied by lavish, upscale props. But beneath his megastar ermine, he was still the same screwed up white boy from Detroit, still buzzing on dope beats, still hanging with the same compadres. One thing had changed. He was no longer boiling with rage against his mom. With all legal matters settled between them, he turned stone cold on her.

WHITE AMERICA

After a (very brief) opening skit, in which the "curtain" rises and Eminem shuffles out and announces himself with a sheepish cough, "White America" strikes up with an almost heavy metal fanfare, as Eminem delivers an awestruck account of his rise to fame. While still streaked with anger and nakedly honest, this is as near as Em ever gets to something like satisfaction: "I'm loving it/I shovelled shit all my life, now I'm dumping it." As the beat rolls mechanically forward, there's Eminem, like a young general at the helm, scarf fluttering, arms crossed, surveying all before him, reflecting on how he got here. Raising his voice to a bellow, louder than we're used to, as if acknowledging the huge assembly he's now addressing, Eminem talks of the legions of fans who share his "beliefs". Even now, Eminem doesn't let ego get the better of him. What he offers here is a realistic assessment of an astonishing campaign to reach the hearts and minds of American youth which has succeeded beyond his wildest expectations.

He knows the impact heavy airplay has had on the American psyche, he knows he's so big even Congress regards him as some sort of threat. And he's unanswerably candid when it comes to assessing the importance of his skin colour: "Let's do the math, if I was black I would have sold half." He knows he's beyond hip hop now. He pays tribute to Dre, the "only one to look past" his Caucasian-ness, but also points out that Dre enjoyed a career upsurge by his association with Eminem and that for every black fan he got, it was only the equivalent of the white fans Dre got – a straight swap.

He mockingly plays up the fears of suburbanites who were happy when rap was confined to Harlem but now see it creeping into their own white heartlands, via Eminem's malign influence. He sarcastically casts himself as a "Derringer aimed at little Erica", before exploding in a final fit of spitting fury at self-appointed censors like Lynne Cheney and Tipper Gore, blue in the face, cursing them with the "freest of speech this Divided States of Embarrassment will allow me to have." His final, chuckling pay-off line – "I'm just playing America, you know I love you" – is about as reassuring as a playful slap on the face from Joe Pesci in *Goodfellas*.

"White America" is a forthright, unflinching and shrewd summary of Eminem's fame and impact. As ever, he doesn't mince his words, yet there's a fundamental irony in the hollered title of the song. He's deriding White America as his

IN SERIAL KILLER GARB FOR A LONDON PERFORMANCE IN 2001

frigid, uptight foe, gathering up its skirts and slapping Advisory stickers on him. However, White America is also where the peroxide-Aryan Eminem draws the greater mass of his fans from. The title's at once a put down but also has the uneasy power of a call to arms among disaffected Caucasian youth.

BUSINESS

Although "Business" is more like vintage Eminem, with its Dre-produced ticking riff and cyclical, bouncing backbeat, again there's a fresh feeling of a mass audience in the house, as well as another grand fanfare (a female chorus eggs him in with coos of "Marshall!") as he hits the mic.

This time out, the conceit is that he and Dre have teamed up like "Saddam and [bin] Laden", or, less threateningly, Batman and Robin ("Holy bat syllables!"), swooping down to blast doors off their hinges and looking to apply some sort of rap enema to a nervous USA. Theirs, he claims, is the biggest duet "since me and Elton played career Russian Roulette." Having emerged alive from that notorious Grammy appearance has evidently made Eminem feel a great deal stronger.

Although boasts are delivered both on his own behalf and Dre's, Em is bolder now in asserting his pre-eminence in the world of hip hop. Once upon a time, all he demanded was some respect. Now he's extolling his own freestyling skills and cockily asserting, "Can't leave rap, the game needs me."

And it's just a tiny bit sad to hear Dre's vocal contributions reduced to the occasional "Hell, yeah!" in the final verse, as if his role has been busted down from that of the respected mentor to the trusty sidekick.

CLEANIN' OUT MY CLOSET

Nothing flip about "Cleanin' Out My Closet". Here, Jeff Bass's intricate, reggaefied backbeat indicates that this is Eminem in thoughtful, serious mode, staring into the flickering embers, brooding intensely on his grievances, chief among these the behaviour of Mrs Mathers-Briggs. And here, for the first time, rather than content himself with sideswipes against his mom, he lyrically grabs her by the lapels and takes her severely and thoroughly to task. It's painful, awful, fascinating. Lines like, "You selfish bitch, I hope you fuckin' burn in hell for this shit" aren't exactly Shakespeare in themselves. Yet as you grasp for comparisons, there is something Shakespearean about the venomous, tear-streaked, inter-familial rage here; the sense of the most basic human link, between mother and child, being horribly, publicly violated.

Eminem's mother, Debbie, had continued to pursue her grievance against her son. She had recorded a rap CD, bitterly alluded to in "Closet", in order to "set the record straight," tell her side of the story. Entitled "Why Are You Doing Me Like You Are", it was a plaintive, pathetic attempt to engage with her son on his own terms, with more than a desperate, tacky whiff of exploitation about it. In interviews, however, she painted herself as a goodly and patient mother wronged, who still loved her son and had only sued him on advice from her lawyer that he needed a "wake-up call" – tough love.

By her account, she was still in touch with Em and that only his need to keep up tough-guy appearances prevented him from exhibiting his more vulnerable and conciliatory attitudes towards his mother in public. Patiently, she spoke of working hard to mend their relationship. If she was at fault, she said, it was in being too solicitous towards young Marshall. "He really had no responsibilities," she said. "I sheltered him too much and I think there's a little resentment from that." Much of his present-day anger she ascribed to the "stress" of working in the music business.

However, while many of those who knew Mrs Mathers-Briggs do indeed remember her as a good and devoted mother, others have hinted at a darker, more erratic side to her character. In 1996, she was taken to court, having been accused by St Clair Shores school officials of abusing her younger son, Eminem's half-brother Nathan. (She later pleaded no contest to reduced charges.) It was suggested that she suffered from Munchausen Syndrome, an affliction whereby mothers deliberately hurt their children so as to gain sympathy and attention for themselves. Although there is some scepticism nowadays about the liberality with which this (hard to disprove) charge has been applied against mothers, especially in America, Eminem pounces on it in "Cleaning Out My Closet": "Victim of Munchausen Syndrome/My whole life I was made to believe I was sick when I wasn't, till I grew up /Now I blew up."

Eminem once again alludes to his mother "popping prescription pills" and "bitching that someone's always going through her purse and shit's missin'." Again, there is corroboration for these charges. One Don DeMarc, who lived with Eminem's mother in the early '70s, states that she made wide use of "pain pills" to counter a myriad of complaints ranging from toothaches to headaches to the long-term effects of a car crash.

As for her paranoia, Mrs Mathers-Briggs was, it seems, constantly involved in ructions with her neighbours, one of whom, according to school officials, she accused of killing her dog in a Satanic ritual. She also suggested that her house was being monitored by video cameras and that an un-named enemy had sent her a tarantula in the mail. Police from St Clair Shores confirmed that she often called them out on what turned out to be unsubstantiated complaints against her neighbours.

A picture emerges from this account of an irrational, self-obsessed woman incapable of giving out real love but nonetheless overbearing. Former employees of the restaurant Eminem worked at remember that she was constantly calling him – and that Eminem spent much of his time crashing at friends rather than go back and endure her company.

If she was indeed the mom from hell, than that is the place to which Eminem consigns her here.

As with "Kim", he doesn't work from a fixed emotional position but ranges across an entire gamut of moods and voices, the confusions and contradictions of which are doubtless a true reflection of his jumbled feelings. He talks early on about his father, absconding from the house when Em was a baby.

He displays a moment of hurt and loss – "I wonder if he ever kissed me goodbye?" – which he abruptly retracts, declaring instead: "I just fuckin' wish he would die." But it's less the absence of a father figure Eminem laments than the hideous presence of the mother figure. On the chorus, which he actually sings, to signify his earnestness he apologizes to his mom, in a "this-hurts-you-more-than-it-hurts-me" sort of way, before solemnly insisting that the matter has to be finally purged from his system, once and for all.

But by the end of the song he's worked himself into a fever of taunting and vengeful jeering. "You're getting older now and it's cold when you're lonely..." he tells her, while telling her that she'll never see Hailie again: "She won't even be at your funeral."

For those that are wondering what even a woman as unbalanced as Eminem's mother could ultimately have done to deserve such lyrical acid

EMINEM'S WORLD TOUR CONFIRMED HIS STATUS AS A PERFORMER.

being thrown in her face, he concludes by dredging up a remark he claims she once made which, if indeed it was made, has burned unforgotten in his soul like a searing hot coal: "Remember when Ronnie died you said you wished it was me?/ Well, guess what, I am dead. Dead to you as can be."

Eventually, Mrs Mathers-Briggs settled her lawsuit for a miserable $1600. Eminem had been determined to face her down with all the considerable resources at his disposal. He's cleaned out the closet here for sure but what's left is a dreadful emptiness. Pathetically, Mrs Mathers-Briggs moved into a condo near her son's new home to be closer to him, but no avail. He'd cut her out of his life. "That's my closure song, I guess," he told *The Face*.

PAYING HOMAGE TO HIS HOMEYS IN A D12 SHIRT, LOS ANGELES 2000.

SQUARE DANCE

The chorus of twangy, 10-gallon do-si-doing prompted some critics to remark that Eminem had been steeped in the Southern-fried hip hop of groups like OutKast, but really this is crude parody, another reminder that Eminem, a creature of hip hop, regarded most forms of white musical culture with distant amusement. And it's that good ol' boy George W Bush he has lined up between the cross-hairs here and whose administration he intends to lay siege to.

Written shortly after the events of September 11 2001 and the subsequent anthrax scare, in which the world's axis seemed momentarily to have tilted dramatically against the West, Eminem's particular concern is that the "army marchin' in back of me" might find themselves drafted into the actual army. Envisaging mass conscription in the wake of the Al-Qaeda atrocities, he scares his fans with visions of being Shanghaied into the services: "You're a baby, gettin' recruited at 18/You're on a plane now, eating their food and baked beans." He doesn't offer much in the way of political prescription and you get the impression that, despite occasional pious protestations to the contrary, 9/11 didn't seismically alter his worldview. All he advises kids to do is, "Stand and fight for the right to say something you might not like," though the geopolitical implications of exercising the democratic right to be a pottymouth are unclear. Needless to say, there was no conscription, which takes the sting out of these verses when viewed retrospectively.

The second object of Eminem's anger here is the rapper Canibus, who had attracted Eminem's ire when he made unauthorized use of the character Stan on his album C True Hollywood Stories. The track "Stan Lives", in which Canibus imagines the hapless Eminem fan being rescued from the water and delivers his own take on matters in an Eminem-style rant, is hardly vicious stuff but Eminem bruises easily. Here, his ripostes are restricted to puns on his name – "Cana-bitch" and "Fan-a-bitch" – with more mainstream fans probably left wondering who on earth Canibus is, let alone what he's done to annoy Eminem. Still, this represents a step up from the rather easy stabs at blow-up doll-style pop targets like Britney Spears, even if Canibus undoubtedly welcomed, rather than was traumatized by, the attention paid to him here.

THE KISS

One of the skits on *The Eminem Show*, in which, against a martial backbeat, Eminem dramatically re-enacts the incident in which he drove out to the Hot Rocks cafe in Warren, Michigan, and caught his wife Kim kissing John Guerra. It bleeds straight into…

SOLDIER

It was a while since the pistol-whipping incident with Kim but you can tell here that even the very recollection of it sets Eminem's blood pumping. After a preface in which he explains that, although he never was a thug, there are so many people out there looking to test the "real" Eminem against the pistol-toting antics of his albums that he has to assume a militaristic position of Bronson-like readiness. So here he is, muscles tensed and twitchy, imagining meting out the sort of punishment he did to Guerra – an example of Slim Shady snaking his way into Em's blood for real, turning him into his own fictional street hood, at least briefly.

Here, as the backbeat churns over and over, he mulls on that scene outside the Hot Rocks cafe, successfully conveying the way his suspicions about what his wife is up to are ticking over in his mind like a time-bomb:

"Listen as the sound ticks on the clock/Listen to the sound of Kim as she licks on a cock." As he strafes the joint with bullets, the targets multiply in his mind, as "damn critics" are mown down in the carnage, along with innocent bystanders, who will go to their graves at least knowing not to underestimate the homicidal intent of a crossed Eminem.

There are danger signs here, which recur occasionally on *The Eminem Show*, of Eminem beginning to succumb to what one critic described as "rock self-importance", forgetting to dab in those touches of lightness that are his forte. Still, they do redeem this track: "I like pissing you off, it gets me off/Like my lawyers, when the fuckin' judge lets me off." Eminem had indeed gotten off the hook for the gun charges that had hung over him since June 2000. Having pleaded no contest in both cases, he was sentenced to a year's probation and fined $2,300 at Oakland County Court.

However, he also had to endure a dressing down, as well as a little gratuitous teasing, from the bench. Judge Denise Langford Morris, playing perhaps to the gallery, listed out loud the punishments members of the public had suggested Eminem undergo, which included "washing his mouth out with soap". In conclusion, she quipped, "Mr Mathers, now is the time for you to please stand up." The line about the "fuckin' judge" was a small, consolatory gesture of revenge for his courtroom belittling. As for John Guerra, who had brought a civil action against Eminem, he would eventually settle for £70,000 out of court.

SAY GOODBYE TO HOLLYWOOD

It's one of Eminem's great strengths that he acknowledges his multiple emotional responses to life and to the numerous sticky situations he finds himself in. Here, in a song written when contemplating what at one point was the very real possibility of a stretch in jail for the Guerra incident, there's none of the macho posturing of "Soldier" and none of the bluff defiance he showed when discussing the subject in a Face interview. "Say Goodbye To Hollywood" sees Eminem – unusually – caught in the grip of something like panic.

He considers what brought him to this pass, a guy who sold 2 million records, screwing up his life "over some female". There's no sympathy for Kim, who "bailed" from their relationship when "shit got heated," but overall, "Say Goodbye To Hollywood" is relatively light on misogyny and heavy on self-excoriation. Against an ominous backbeat and male voice choir oddly reminiscent of the rolling soundtrack to "Who Wants To Be A Millionaire", Eminem tells himself , "I need to slow down, try to get my feet on solid ground." Right now, life is too much for him to bear. He's reduced to taking solace in comic books. He toys with the idea of suicide but pulls back when he reminds himself of his daughter Hailie, the one thing in his life that's untainted and simple, his sole reason for carrying on. As he discusses his father, and his fear of "growing up to be like his fuckin' ass," we get a glimpse of just why being a good parent is so important to Eminem. It was something he never felt he had himself.

In verse three, the anxiety and regret escalates. He vows never again to go near guns. He curses the life he has chosen, or which his talent chose for him, for putting him in the scrape he's in today. Why did he have to rap? "What about math, how come I was never good at that?" he says. Given his time over, he vows he would never have rapped. He even echoes his most censorious critics, stating that he's "sold his soul to the devil" and that his hip hop career has led him not to glamour and good fortune but down a dark maze. All he wants now is to get out, "level head intact". Hence, he's saying goodbye to Hollywood, the good life, the girl in his arms, the happy ending because, despite all his success and riches, his life was never going to end up that way. "Please don't cry for me/When I'm gone for good," he wails, though he's more likely to be alluding to early retirement rather than suicide.

As things turned out, Eminem needn't have felt so despondent. However, he chooses to include the track here as an important and vivid emotional snapshot of his life and as a means of exhibiting his curse-marks, marks of authenticity and woe, which keep him "real".

DRIPS

A ribald and faintly noxious bit of black comedy this, a twisted descendant of George Clinton's sleazy funk set against a funereal, literally dripping backbeat. It features Obie Trice, previously responsible for the single "The Well Known Asshole", and it's a morality-free morality tale about the dangers of sexually transmitted disease, full of morbid details which are calculated to make the average hip hopster guffaw and grimace. Obie obliges with the first verse, a graphic account of a one-off sexual dalliance which ends with the "bitch" in question upping sticks early the next morning without a goodbye. Naturally, such a "fuck 'em and chuck 'em" attitude is anathema to any self-respecting rap dude and Obie is suitably outraged at her infidelity. He's more concerned, however, that he had unprotected sex and now, thanks entirely to the female, he's had bad news from the doctor.

Eminem takes over for the next verse, full of lyrical loathing for his girlfriend, who he's discovered has been seeing someone else, "sucking his dick and kissing yours when she gets back". It's when it dawns on Em that he's left himself open to the horrors of sexually transmitted disease that you practically see his bottom lip wobbling. "You feel like you've been sticking your dick in a hearse."

Finally, with the Doctor having apparently confirmed AIDS, Em thrashes about in vengeful anguish, the pay-off being that the guy his girlfriend has been seeing is none other than Obie. "This ho's a genius, she g'd us," he cries, with what borders on grudging admiration.

Interesting, here, the contrast between the two rappers. The line "work that nigga like a slave owner" could never have come from Eminem, always impeccably scrupulous in matters racial, but it's OK coming from Obie Trice. Also, while Trice's response to his disease effectively amounts to an irritated "damn", Eminem's more willing to give vent to his fear and let you know he's crapping himself.

WITHOUT ME

Against what sounds like a soundclash of Michael Jackson's "Billie Jean" and Malcolm McClaren's "Buffalo Gals", Eminem goes into Slim Shady/ringmaster mode here, in the sort of light-but-lethal piece of pop/rap which made this an obvious candidate for a single, skipping around the ring, merrily poking his enemies in the eye.

"Without Me" was the first the world would have heard of him in some time. Meanwhile, his various detractors had filled many column inches and airwaves fulminating against him. First up, he takes a deliciously cheap crack at Lynne Cheney, referring to the "heart complications" of her husband, now Vice President Dick Cheney, whose serial coronary problems had left many of the electorate wondering if he was physically fit enough for high office. He snaps at MTV which, having initially supported Eminem, disassociated itself from him when the heat came down from the various lobbies protesting against his lyrics. And, for good measure, there's a big, emancipated "Fuck you!" to his mother Debbie, whose threat of legal action no longer hung over him.

All of which may be more exhilarating than edifying but amid all the poison and popcorn here are some highly salient points. "Without Me" again demonstrates that when it comes to analysis of the Eminem phenomenon, no one is shrewder or sharper than the man himself. He's aware, for instance, of how well the Slim Shady character goes down; he's seen the returns. So "this is what I'll give ya", he says, not just obliging us but playing on our sweet tooth for scandal. He gives a capsule analysis of his success – white kids bored of rock until Eminem comes along, "on a mission and yells 'bitch'!"

"On a mission" is an interesting way of putting it, but it's not that Eminem wants to spread some gospel of misogyny. More he wants to put a rocket up the ass of the left/right coalition of political correctness/moral panic, both of whom are scandalized by… that word! That word which he must not say, but which, the more he's told not to say it, the more he will. Bitch, bitch, bitch! Lenny Bruce would argue that Eminem's repeated use of the word is not only healthy for free speech and the body politic – better out than in – but that, through repetition, it loses its scary potency, becomes exposed as just a syllable. Eventually, at any rate. But in the meantime, it still earns Eminem millions of dollars and worldwide exposure.

Then there's the keynote line in which Eminem remarks how "empty" it feels without him. This is the sharpest observation of the lot. It isn't just his fans for whom life feels empty when Em's inactive but the anti-Eminem brigade also.

He's aware that, for all their sincerity and self-righteousness, the Lynne Cheneys, GLAAD and so forth are galvanized by Eminem. They secretly enjoy the energy surge that comes from rounding on him and bask in the warm feelings of indignation. Eminem gets them out and shouting, gives them a moral purpose. Without him, their lives would be lacking something too. For a supposed homophobe, Eminem adds greatly to the gaiety of nations.

MOBY TRIGGERED YET ANOTHER EMINEM FEUD WHEN HE CRITICIZED THE RAPPER FOR BEING A BAD INFLUENCE ON YOUNGER FANS.

There follows a series of slaps against his pop foes, ranging from Chris Kirkpatrick of N'Sync, who had the temerity to answer back to Em's numerous "disses" on *The Marshall Mathers LP*, to Limp Bizkit, because their DJ Lethal took the side of House Of Pain rapper Everlast in a war of words between him and Em the previous year, and Moby, who had been outspoken in his attacks on Eminem's misogynistic and homophobic lyrics.

Moby presents him with a slightly puzzling target. Eminem loves hip hop but has no real affinity for techno, which, he claims here, "nobody listens to". It's unlikely that Moby would have been wounded by that particular dart, having recently sold some 10 million copies worldwide of his album *Play*.

In the video for "Without Me" (which also featured Dick Cheney being electrocuted) Moby is depicted as being assaulted by a rabbit. Onstage, during the Anger Management tour of 2002, Eminem also "executed" Moby in effigy.

Still, Moby seems to have been somewhat flattered by all this adversity. Writing on his official website, he claimed to be "honoured" to have received his "first celebrity diss" via the rapper. He told Eminem, "If you're reading this, thanks… Really, I mean it. And no hard feelings from me." However, when Moby realized he'd checked into a hotel where Eminem was using the roof terrace for a video shoot he swiftly checked out again for "reasons of personal security".

Eminem's much more acute when satirically taking on board the criticism that he is a "white Elvis", getting rich off black music. Oh yes, he sneers, I'm the worst. But then, what about all of the other "20 million white rappers" who have emerged? None of them have made the same impact as Eminem: "No matter how many fish in the sea it'd still be empty without me." Eminem didn't get huge because he was white but because he brought something raw, fresh and shocking to popular music. We should know that. He certainly does.

PAUL ROSENBERG

A 22-second skit in which Eminem's manager warns him about bringing his gun to the studio and firing it off outside. Followed immediately by…

SING FOR THE MOMENT

After the Slim-sharp "Without Me", "Sing For The Moment" catches Eminem at his most grandiose and even regal – his use of the royal "we" throughout this lyric is interesting. This is a heartfelt but at times almost pompous tribute to himself, couched in billowing, sub-heavy metal tones and sampling Aerosmith's "Dream On" for its chorus. When Aerosmith had formed a rap-metal coalition with Run-DMC on "Walk This Way" it had taken the music into the stratosphere, so it's fitting that Eminem should tip his hat to Steven Tyler here. Tyler's lyric is essentially an injunction not to put off enjoying and celebrating life to the full because tomorrow "the good Lord may take you away". It's a powerful, chest-surging sentiment which makes for a swollen crescendo.

Eminem begins by painting a damning picture of a young adolescent growing up in a repressive household where "no swearing" is allowed. In his own headphone zone, the kid "talks back, talks black, brainwashed by rap and metal". This puritanical household then somehow metamorphoses into one in which the kid is living with an abusive stepfather, in a "broken home" where there's "no control", so he allows his emotions to let rip. Whatever, the result is the same – these kids "worship" Eminem and hang on his every word, an idea which causes the rapper a moment of unease. Toying with the notion that words can "teach hate", Eminem wonders that these kids "hang on every single statement they make". After all, it's not so long ago that Eminem was one of those kids himself. Eminem then turns on his persecutors, ranging from critics and ex-fans to the police and judges who oppress him even as they're having him sign CDs for their kids. Eminem marvels at the absurdity that he is considered an outlaw. "If I'm a criminal, how the fuck can I raise a little girl?" he protests. This probably wouldn't be the best time to remind us of his actual criminal misdeeds but Em can't resist doing so in a digressive sideswipe to John Guerra: "That was a fist that hit you!"

Although his fans hang on his every word, Eminem mocks the idea that his lyrics have any real power of suggestion. "If it can, the next time you assault a dude, just tell the judge it was my fault and I'll get sued," he jeers.

The closing lines are the most touching, as Eminem talks about the disenfranchised kids out there with "nothing but a dream and a rap magazine", although the more misty-eyed he gets about them, "crying at night, wishing he could die," the more inflated, sentimental and uncharacteristically po-faced his rhymes become. "Just let our spirits live on, through our lyrics that you hear in our songs," he emotes. Fortunately, the outtro kicks in, otherwise Eminem might have spiralled upwards into still dizzier realms of guff.

Although "Sing For The Moment" doesn't bear close lyrical inspection, if you get caught in the emotion of this song, it's soul-stirring and air-punching stuff and it's as near as Eminem gets to the headiness of stadium rock.

SUPERMAN

Over a slinky, funk-saturated groove, Eminem engages in some sexy back-and-forth with vocalist Dina Rae, who coos and groans as they make out. Just as they're getting really intimate, however, Eminem snaps his head back. He's only recently gotten out of the relationship with Kim – "no ring on this finger now" – and aggressively sends out a stark blast of lyrical "bitch"– epellent to any wily female who's thinking of getting in among him and taking her place. That's the last thing he needs right now. Naturally, there are plenty of willing candidates out there – he is, after all, "Superman", able to "leap tall hos in single bound". But beyond a quick roll in the hay, they've no chance. "Kiss my dick, get my cash?" Eminem don't think so. For Mariah Carey, Eminem concedes he might make an exception, but the rest can "just sit your drunk ass on the runway" and take off.

Worse are the women who try to inveigle themselves into Eminem's personal life by trying to flatter him with sweet-talk about the things that mean the most to him, including his daughter Hailie. "Don't grow partial… I'll slap you off that barstool." The testosterone swimming in his head now exciting thoughts of violence rather than sex, he winds up unable to resist a rhyme of "tampax" and "anthrax", threatening to insert the latter into the errant "ho" via the former. "Superman" was written in the panicky period following 9/11 when a spate of anthrax mailshots convinced the nation that bin Laden was attempting to poison them one by one via the post office. The cases soon subsided and were later concluded to have been the work of a disgruntled American scientist. Although "Superman" is pretty nasty stuff, the emotional undercurrent is plain enough – Em's fear of commitment. This isn't exactly Simon & Garfunkel's "I Am A Rock". Eminem refuses to hint outright here that he would be so weak as to put himself in emotional thrall to another woman. Not "Superman". However, the aggressiveness with which he wards off all "hos" suggests that deep down he knows he's all too capable of doing so.

It's ironic that, given lines like "bitches they come and go", Eminem has demonstrated immense professional fidelity to Dina Rae, to whom he invariably turns when needing a female vocal. Some might argue that this is because few women could stand Eminem's misogynistic company, but it's more likely that Eminem is, unusually for such a huge pop celebrity, extraordinarily constant in his loyalty to his old friends.

HAILIE'S SONG

Set to a rock-a-bye, trip-hoppy groove, "Hailie's Song" sees Eminem make his debut as a full-on vocalist. And it's fair to say that he takes to singing like a cat to water – not well. He admits as much: "I can't sing – but I feel like singing." And after inflicting two verses of heartfelt, torturous vocals, as appealing as the sound of balloons bring rubbed up and down jumpers, he concedes defeat. "If I could hit the notes I'd blow something as long as my father."

Wavering unsteadily in the upper registers like an inexperienced hang glider, Eminem reflects with dewy eyes on his daughter, the "only lady that I adore" and the one person he lives for. Yet he can't help getting pulled back into melancholy and bitterness. Feeling the "weight of the world on my shoulders" he has to remind himself continually that he has Hailie, source of all his pride, whom he watches grow up day by day with great fondness and love. But then his mood turns from pink to black as he starts dwelling on Kim, whose infidelities and neglect still make his blood boil. "I've been to bat for this woman," he protests, entirely glossing over the verbal battings he also administered to her on "'97 Bonnie & Clyde" and "Kim". Finally he calms down again and loses himself in the sort of touching but mushy talk that's probably best left to father and daughter at tucking-in time. Still, inevitable lines like "What did I stick my penis up in?" break up the tendency here towards drivelling squishiness nicely.

STEVE BERMAN

A reprise of the skit on *The Marshall Mathers EP*, performed again by Steve Berman, Interscope's senior executive of marketing and sales. Last time, Berman kicked Eminem out of his office with a flea in his ear about how he couldn't sell his album. On this occasion, when summoned, Eminem has come prepared for a repeat performance. Just as Berman's launching into his rant – "This is by far the most…" – Eminem shoots him where he stands, only for Berman to gurgle, with his dying breath the second part of the sentence – "…the most incredible thing I have ever heard."

WHEN THE MUSIC STOPS

Amid the tinny, synthetic rhythms and rock flourishes prevalent on much of *The Eminem Show*, it's good to savour the fresh grits of the Southern boogie backbeat on this track. Eminem is joined once more by the various members of his old posse, D12. After warming up with some gangsta freestyling, Em gets down to the topic in hand, slipping from cartoon to reality as he muses, "This is crap, this ain't rap when we confuse hip hop/with real life when the music stops."

Most of the members of D12 depart entirely from their brief, Swifty and Von bigging themselves up as the hardest niggas on the block; Kon Artis musing morosely on the pratfalls of stardom, the friends you lose, the hangers-on you gain. Only Bizarre tackles the motion proposed by Eminem, sardonically depicting himself as a gullible sop for every musical trend of the past 15 years – from obeying NWA's "Fuck Tha Police" rule of thumb and landing up in jail, to dying his hair blue and "growing titties" after listening to Marilyn Manson.

SAY WHAT U SAY

An Eminem/Dr Dre duet this, with the latter providing a lurching backbeat, peg-legging menacingly towards you like a mummy in a '50s horror movie. "Say What You Say" is primarily given over to Dr Dre's beef against Atlanta-based So So Def CEO/producer Jermaine Dupri, who had first come to rap prominence with his work with juvenile duo Kriss Kross. "Say What U Say" is an example of how even relatively innocuous-sounding remarks in interviews can lead, in hip hop, to bruised feelings and bruising vendettas. Dupri had happened to mention in an interview that he couldn't understand why he wasn't bracketed alongside Dre and Timbaland in the pantheon of great producers. This infuriated Dre and egged on by Eminem ("What about Jermaine?") he moves to put down the upstart Dupri here. "Over 80 million albums sold/And I ain't have to do it with 10 or 11-year-olds," he sneers, in reference to Kriss Kross.

Eminem offers backup here and, in a manner more reminiscent of a Victorian clubman dealing with a particularly irksome bounder, threatens to "blackball" any hip hoppers who cross him. Finally, Timbaland himself joins the anti-Dupri chorus with a curt "suck my dick".

Dupri was swift to answer back in his next release, deriding Dre as a "same beat-making, non-rapping individual" and pouring contempt on Eminem's attacks on easy pop targets. "To me, you like a character in Disney World/ Known for dissing pop groups and Justin's ex-girl/Shit, don't nobody take you serious."

TILL I COLLAPSE

Featuring the slick tones of G-Funk vocalist Nate Dogg (who'd previously appeared alongside Warren G on his massive hit "Regulate"), "Till I Collapse" is a death-or-glory broadside from Eminem, heavily sampling the martial, stomp-rock rhythms of Queen's "We Will Rock You". Not the most original of musical ideas, one which American sports had long since cottoned onto, but as ever with Eminem, the real business is in the rhymes.

Here he comes on as angry as Yosemite Sam as he once again reflects at length on his career, status, impact and what he sees as the lack of respect afforded to him. He recognizes that he's the "cause of a lot of envy" in the business and witheringly acknowledges that he's the "press's wet dream, like Bobby and Whitney" – Bobby Brown and Whitney Houston, whose volatile relationship and increasingly strung-out private lives made them prime *National Enquirer* fodder. All of that, though, is clouding judgment of his true credentials.

On the one hand he's looking to be counted alongside his rap heroes and peers, including "Jay-Z, Tupac and Biggie" and the boys from OutKast, while on the other he's adopting the more amplified tones of stadium rock, realising that his constituency now extends way beyond the bounds of hip hop. From starting off feeling like he's on the edge of collapse, by the end of this rap he's pumped himself up into the conviction that "no one can beat me". This sort of pep-talking would become an increasingly prominent feature of his lyrical style.

MY DAD'S GONE CRAZY

Featuring the sampled vocals of daughter Hailie Jade, by now six years old, this could have been a fatherly indulgence too far, especially after the borderline "Hailie's Song" earlier on. In fact, it's a brilliant finale to the album. All the various strands of Eminem – love of his daughter, hate of his mom, sly, twinkling self-deprecation, black-as-tar angst, advanced rapology and scatology, all come at you here in one great, bouncing bundle, to an orchestral backdrop which faintly and appropriately reminds you of the theme to The Addams Family. Hailie's vocal interventions, including her excited and curiously accented holler of the song title, could have been sickly-cute. Yet somehow they're almost disturbing, the way they're looped into the mix. Maybe that and the fact that dad gives every evidence of being more than Halloween-mask scary. "No one can save me, not even Hailie," he admits, consigning himself still further beyond the pale than ever before.

"I'm going to hell, who's coming with me?" he announces at the start, like he's proposing a trip to Disneyland. And then, the ride begins, with Hailie giggling and gurgling along, adding the odd chainsaw sound effect. Though she wouldn't have been present for Em's profanity-laced outpourings, there's still something exhilaratingly dubious about her being on the track at all.

Eminem rises to inspired heights of invective as he parodies his mother's whining: "Rana rana rana rana rana rana rana rana… if you ain't got nuthin' nice to say then don't say nuthin'." Not for Eminem: "I'd rather be a pussy whipped bitch, eat pussy and have pussy lips glued to my face with a clit ring in my nose," he declares.

The ante of appallingness is upped several times. He claims to have been having unprotected sex with Dr Dre. Identifying once again with anti-hero bin Laden, he threatens to blow everything off the map "except Afghanistan". But it's towards the end of the song that the lyrical storm clouds really start to gather and, completely out of kilter with the exuberant mood of the song, Eminem extravagantly compares his pain to that of a little girl on board a plane about to crash into the World Trade Center. He revisits again the misery of standing at his Uncle Ronnie's grave, grieving the loss of the one familial lodestar in his life, a tragedy which pierced his very soul and left him utterly embittered, not least against the surviving women in his life. Far from holding back and delivering a junior version of himself here, Em deliberately catapults himself as far into the black as he can go. "I wouldn't let Hailie listen to me neither," he says at the conclusion. This isn't a tacked-on copout but Eminem being true to the decency that's as big a part of himself as any other. It's also an indication of how damned he considers himself to be.

EMINEM AND HIS MANAGER PAUL ROSENBERG AT THE 2003 DETROIT HIP HOP SUMMIT.

8 MILE

For years prior to the US 2000 release of *8 Mile*, there had been talk of Eminem breaking into movies. If he was wary, that was understandable. Other pop icons, ranging from Vanilla Ice to Madonna, had bombed laughably at the box office, while fellow hip hop stars like Snoop Doggy Dogg had not made the transition well either. Indeed, Eminem had already made unheralded and best-forgotten cameo appearances. There was 2001's *The Wash*, a poor remake of *Car Wash* starring Dre and Dogg, in which Em appeared briefly as a psychotic telephone stalker, as well as a straight-to-video spoof horror project, *The Hip hop Witch*. He had also been courted for the role of rookie sidekick to Denzel Washington in 2001's *Training Day* but he backed out – the part went to Ethan Hawke.

The notion of *8 Mile* had been born during a conversation between Hollywood producer Brian Grazer and Interscope head Jimmy Iovine, the man who had been co-responsible for launching Em's musical career. They had in mind a 21st century project that would do for hip hop what *Saturday Night Fever* had done for disco in the 1970s. Although conventionally associated with strobe lights, white suits and the white teeth of the brothers Gibb, *Fever* had actually been quite a street-tough project, written by an old US socialist Norman Wexler and only partly sanitized for screen consumption. After some initial reluctance, Eminem quickly agreed to the project.

After putting out feelers to a number of mainstream directors, Grazer decided to go with Curtis Hanson, a safe pair of hands who was capable nonetheless of crafting quality work – he had directed *LA Confidential* and *Wonder Boys*. Hanson and Eminem visited Detroit together. Hanson was ostensibly there to scout for locations but he was also there to make up his mind about whether Eminem was up to the task of a major starring role. When he saw the way he bonded with his many fans and greeters in Detroit, however, he recognized that Eminem still had a link and an affinity with the place where he grew up that superstardom hadn't extinguished. So long as the movie was filmed in Detroit – there had been studio plans to film it in the more blockbuster-friendly ghettos of New York or LA – Eminem would be cool.

Once filming got underway, not everyone greeted Eminem so warmly, however. Angry locals turned up at the shoot waving placards carrying the slogan, "SLIM SHADY GO HOME!" There were objections raised by local Detroit councillors to a scene in which a house is burned to the ground. When Councillor Earl O Wheeler Jr was interviewed, it became clear that it was as much Eminem he objected to as the fake arson. "What Eminem stands for is the antithesis of what I stand for," he said.

Em's patience snapped when another band of protesters emerged from Warren, the Detroit suburb he'd grown up in, indignant that he was giving the district a bad name. "A bad name? The fucking white trash capital of the world? Shut the fuck up!" was his response.

The cinematography of Mexican cameraman Rodrigo Prieto would ensure that the washed up, derelict, post-industrial streets of Detroit would determine the adverse and downbeat mood of the movie, a compelling and ultimately inspiring saga but one relatively short on light relief – high on rags, low on riches.

Set in 1995, Eminem plays Jimmy "Rabbit" Smith, a wannabe white rapper not unlike Eminem himself at that time – dirt poor, yet to go peroxide, with an allegedly pregnant girlfriend, Janeane, who's just dumped him, working a lousy day job at a pressing plant in what's left of Detroit's motor industry and trying to meet a deadline for his rap career to go off.

We see him in the dismal bathroom of the Shelter, the dank venue where 45-second rap battles take place, hosted by Future (ER's Mekhi

EMINEM AND *8-MILE* CO-STAR BRITANNY MURPHY IN A SCENE FROM THE MOVIE.

EMINEM AS 'RABBIT' PSYCHES HIMSELF UP FOR ANOTHER RAP BATTLE.

Phifer), a member of Eminem's crew. He's desperately trying to nail down his rhymes and his moves, but he hasn't got it together inside and, after vomiting just before he's due onstage, he freezes traumatically at the mic, an event he must spend the remainder of the movie living down and, finally, making amends for.

Rabbit draws largely, but not entirely, on Em's own experiences. Like Em, he grows up in a trailer park. Rabbit's mother, played by Kim Basinger, is an alcoholic, pathetically clinging to her weekly bingo and an abusive partner, Rabbit's "stepdaddy". Rabbit also has a six-year-old sister, Lily, upon whom he lavishes the sort of sweet affection Eminem gives his own daughter Hailie. Rabbit drives around in a beat-up car and, early on, he and his crew have fun cruising around town, shooting paintballs, much as Eminem had in his youth.

This celluloid version of Eminem, however, is, overall, a great deal more sympathetic and acceptable to mainstream sensibilities than the various Eminem personae put over on record. Frankly, it has to be, for the film to work at all. Far from being homophobic, there's a scene in which Eminem defends a gay man in the workplace. It feels rather contrived and tacked on and suggests Em was more affected by criticisms from groups like GLAAD than he let on. Yet it also points up a plausible aspect of Eminem that he often obscures himself with his lyrical outbursts of self-aggrandizement – that his instinct is to stick up for the underdog.

As for misogyny, it has to be said that Kim Basinger plays Eminem's mother as a deeply flawed but a rounded and eventually sympathetic figure, much more so than the ogress Em depicts on songs like "Cleanin'

Out My Closet". Indeed, there's a faint crackle of Oedipal energy in their scenes together – Em even asked Basinger to autograph his copy of *9½ Weeks* during the shoot. Janeane, the "Kim" equivalent here, played by singer Taryn Manning, is fickle and slimy, a "bitch" sure enough but she appears only fleetingly. More screen time is given to Eminem's on/off relationship with Alex, an aspiring model played by Brittany Murphy, the sort of assertive, independent but essentially decent woman who never features in any of Slim Shady's rants against "bitches" or "hoes". The mutual respect, if not quite love, which they develop, is one of the more subtle aspects of *8 Mile*.

Furthermore, *8 Mile* is conspicuously lacking in gangsta action. There's the tomfoolery involving paintballs, there's some dissing and shoving and a couple of beatings. However, when Cheddar Bob, the dumbest member of Rabbit's crew (a lobotomized Eminem) produces a gun during an altercation with a rival posse, the gasp of horror and surprise that spreads through the group is similar to what might be expected if Ross were suddenly to pull out a revolver in Central Perk in *Friends*: "My Gaad! put it away!"

This is "nice" Eminem, an Eminem everyone can root for. "Bitches" can drink in his broody, blue-eyed sensitivity, "fags" can be assured that they have no truer friend than Rabbit. Yet, strangely, it would be wrong to talk of Rabbit as a "sanitized" Eminem. Rabbit is almost certainly truer to the actual Marshall Mathers, than, say, the level-headed character Tupac Shakur played in *Gridlock'd* was to the headstrong Tupac of real life. Em plays Rabbit with a subdued naturalness, not overly demonstrative emotionally but deceptively dead-eyed, clearly internally bruised by the sneers and tribulations heaped on him during *8 Mile*, taking things in, storing things up.

It's with the last 20 minutes of the movie that *8 Mile* really bursts into life, with the final, glorious, gladiatorial rap showdown. One by one, a galvanized Em picks off his opponents and wins over the (mostly) black crowd. Finally, he meets his earlier nemesis, Wink. Forced to go up first, he delivers his final, brilliant rap masterstroke. He preempts all the disses Wink has in store for him, admits all his weaknesses, shouts out that he's trailer trash – but still he's standing there. This, of course, is above all else the secret of Eminem's success, what makes him untouchable in rap. He exposes himself (literally too, baring his white ass) in a way few, if any, of his rap peers are prepared to. And sure enough, Wink has no answer. It's his turn to freeze – especially as Eminem is able to reveal that Wink's street credentials are bogus. He's an upper middle class slummer. He might have the right skin colour but Eminem has the truer street pedigree.

That last revelation may have been a convenient twist too far in the plot but it doesn't ruin an immensely satisfying climax to *8 Mile*. The ending is all the better for not catapulting Rabbit to the same superstar status as Eminem. Victorious in the rap battle, he goes back and finishes his shift at the factory – keeping it real. This dismayed one or two critics, including Roger Ebert who, in an otherwise laudatory review, crustily wondered aloud, "What has happened to our hopes, that young audiences now embrace such cheerless material, avoiding melody like the plague?" There were one or two dissenting voices, too. Peter Bradshaw in the *Guardian* criticized Eminem for what he saw as his screen absence, a certain emotional neutrality. Generally, however, Em's performance was well-received – one writer anointed him the "hip hop James Dean". Eminem himself simply said, "I just wanted to make an authentic movie about the place where I grew up."

Eminem found the collaborative process of shooting the film stressful, despite director Hanson's warnings. "I told him how long and difficult the process would be," said Hanson. "I wanted him to know, because I didn't want him to enter into it lightly. And as frank as I was, he still didn't really get it." But by the time it wrapped Em was already sniffing around for future projects.

It was for his musical contribution, however, that Eminem would be awarded an Oscar. As executive producer, he was responsible for overseeing the soundtrack, to which he contributed three numbers himself and collaborated on two others. Billed as music from and inspired by the film (which half-excuses the fact that much of it has nothing to do with the film), the soundtrack was a chance for him not only to enable his old posse D12 to take another musical bow, but also to showcase some of the new acts he'd signed to his own label, Shady Records.

These included Obie Trice, whose "Adrenaline Rush" positively drips sonic testosterone as he showers himself in boastful glory, giving full vent to his "toxic tonsils" and delivering an eyebrow-raising namecheck to a British celebrity chef: "I cook up that hot shit like Ainsley Harriot!"

50 Cent, whose gangsta credentials were well established and who would go on to rival Eminem in the superstar stakes, has two tracks here. "Places To Go" opens with ritual threats of gunshot wounds before he

MUCH OF THE MOVIE *8-MILE* HAS BEEN ACKNOWLEDGED AS BEING AUTOBIOGRAPHICAL FOR EMINEM.

settles into a slick but lethal line of funky patter, even mock-slurring his lines as he relishes a bottle of Dom Perignon. On "Wanksta", with an almost amused contempt, he chides fellow MCs who lack his own, fearsome background and who bring nothing to the rap party: "You say you a gangsta but you never pop nothing."

Jay-Z and Nas, the two New York rappers who were locked in an interminable feud, both appear on the soundtrack here. Jay-Z teams up with Freeway, his own cool delivery contrasting with some seriously overheated blather on the mic from the latter. Nas, meanwhile, to the weariness of many critics, chooses to have a go at Jay-Z on "You Wanna Be Me". He doesn't need to mention him in person – their war of words was well-known enough for everyone to know to whom "faggot, bitch, you coward, you clown" is addressed. Oddly enough, in interviews, Nas seemed the more reluctant to pursue the quarrel, but an MTV poll declared Nas the victor over Jay-Z in the diss-stakes – by 52% to 48%. Xzibit, sometime collaborator with Eminem, delivers some nasty rhymes over a buzzing, electro-reggae backdrop: "Every time I spit, I shine."

A few of the old(er) school get an airing here under Eminem's curatorship. Rakim, for instance, who alongside Eric B was responsible for some of the most erudite and razor-sharp lines of early hip hop. A creature of a syllabically virtuoso but pre-gangsta rap era, he modestly compares his return to that of "Jesus to the ghetto", but then gets mighty mystical, describing himself as "close by every spirit that never made it to birth". Gang Starr (the duo Guru and DJ Premier), also of late '80s vintage, show they still can cut it and cut the new generations of aspirants to size: "You had one single but then your album sounds wack." Young Zee, who wrote Pras' part for the Fugees' "Ready Or Not", chimes in with the weak "That's My Niggas 4 Real", the (unusual) gist of which is that he doesn't give a damn whether he sells records as he makes enough money selling drugs on the street.

Macy Gray's rather limp "Time Of My Life" doesn't really cut it here. Coming on as ever like a husky hybrid of Aretha Franklin and Donald Duck, she introduces a change of pace and mood that fails to refresh. Brother-and-sister group Boomkast, featuring Taryn Manning (who appears in *8 Mile*) doesn't sit well in this overbearingly macho company either. The romantically strained trip-hop sounds way too precious and uptown for this company.

LOSE YOURSELF

Eminem wrote this during the hectic weeks in which the movie *8 Mile* was made. It's the song that rolls over the closing credits; the song, we are to assume, which Rabbit has been composing, scribbling on scraps of paper at every opportunity during the film. Said director Curtis Hanson, "I had an opportunity, as a lover of music in movies, to do something unique. We showed an artist struggling to create, saw him putting down words and heard fragments of a beat, and then at the end, when the character had found his voice, we heard a full-blown version of the song, performed by the artist we had just watched creating it. I didn't know of any other movie that was able to do that."

Musically, from its melancholy intro to the pump of the ignition as the rhythm kicks in like a rapid heartbeat, this is Eminem at his absolute finest. He deservedly won an Oscar in 2003 for Best Original Song, seeing off competition from U2. "Lose Yourself" encapsulates not just the events of *8 Mile*, but the pulsating inner drive which has been beating away inside Rabbit, ever since he first froze. As first the keyboards, then the bass, crank up the adrenaline, he relives the prickly humiliation of the crowd jeering, the vomit stinking up his sweater, hitting the syllables like he's hitting his forehead against a wall. But as his heart keeps beating, veins throbbing, his mind keeps racing. His blood's up and he goes "back to the lab", his trailer park, to do what has to be done.

By the chorus, he's all evangelical and exhorting us to grab life by the tail while we can: "You only get one shot, do not miss your chance to blow/ This opportunity". The way each of Em's phrases spill over into the next line, with no natural pauses, means his verbal energy never lets up.

Eminem doesn't permit any release, however. By the second verse he's a superstar but that doesn't offer any relief from the struggle. "It only grows harder, only grows hotter," as does the beat, jumping regularly into the red as Em realizes that this relentless process is casting him adrift, the outboard motor won't cut out and now "He's grown farther from home, he's no father/He goes home and barely knows his own daughter." And still "the beat goes on."

By the third verse, he slips back in time, brooding and simmering: "I was playing in the beginning, the mood all changed." Then he leaps out of the movie frame, with a quick name-check to his co-star: "There's no Mekhi

Phifer this is my life." Now he's back in the mid-'90s for real, Rabbit for real, reliving the "baby mama drama" of his early marital years, feeling life closing in on him, then deciding that unless he makes it, life's becoming so desperate he'll probably wind up in jail. "Success is my only muthafuckin' option, failure's not," asserts Eminem. There's no modest but stable family and career future for him. If he doesn't make it, he's going to wind up in trailer park hell, in Salem's Lot, a Stephen King white trash nightmare. And so, screwing up every fibre of courage, determination and nerve in his body, he launches himself to make his grab for "the only opportunity that I got."

It might just have been narrative slackness that made Eminem put the second verse before the third, when they might have worked better the other way round. Or it might have been his cheerless way of stating that even when you're winning, it doesn't feel much different to when you were losing. "Eye Of The Tiger" this ain't. Whatever, this is the only possible flaw in a song that perfectly captures the fraught, compulsive rhythms of Eminem's life and work like no other.

LOVE ME

123

LUIS RESTO, CO-WRITER OF "LOSE YOURSELF" ACCEPTING THE AWARD FOR BEST SONG AT THE 2003 OSCARS.

Eminem makes up a trio here with his two protegés, Obie Trice and 50 Cent. The sober, mildly haunting synth string loop and the sweet, unaccredited female chorus line are at tasteful odds with the locker-room boorishness of the lyrics. Trice heckles with lines like, "We wanna love alcohol, we wanna love guns… we don't wanna love bitches though," while 50 Cent pulls the pigtails of every black female star he can call to mind, from Ashanti to Li'l Kim and Lauryn Hill, whom he used to like until, "the bitch put out a CD that didn't have no beat."

Eminem redeems the exercise a little, comparing the lyrical agitation he induces to "trying to smoke crack and go to sleep" and then, more puzzlingly, "I'm the equivalent of what would happen if [George W] Bush rapped." That not quite thought-through line is indicative of an Eminem not exactly straining every sinew.

8 MILE

Eminem goes solo, rapping to the inventive, clickety click railtrack rhythms he and co-writer and programmer Luis Resto lay down here. Eminem oversaw the musical side of the soundtrack to 8 Mile, and here's more evidence of how well he acquitted himself.

Crammed with details from the movie, this is Eminem in his role as Rabbit, riding the bus, turning things over in his mind, reliving being "stripped of his manhood" when he froze at the mic, dreaming vague but desperate dreams of standing up to "travel new land" and "take matters into my own hands", even contemplating abandoning his faithful posse, who, he's tempted to feel, are dragging him back. He's living, literally, on the wrong side of the tracks. There's some particularly poignant lines: "Ain't following no footsteps/I'm making my own."

He also revisits some of the film's most tender and heartwrenching images. For example, he depicts Rabbit's six-year-old sister drawing doodles of innocence as an escape from the hideous domestic experience of living in the trailer, while vicious domestic quarrels and fist-fights break out among the grown-ups: "Colours until the crayon gets dull in her hand… /Ain't no telling what goes on in her little head." As with his own daughter Hailie, you feel Eminem wishes he could somehow preserve her innocence inviolate, having lost his own at such an early age.

THE GANG STARR RAPPER GURU, WHO RAPS ON THE MOVIE SOUNDTRACK.

These rhymes are closer to the beat-up lamentations of the blues than conventional hip hop, as he talks about looking like a bum, cold and miserable, serving MCs at lunchtime, feeling like "another crab in the bucket", helpless in his quest to advance his career. Only near the end does he finally muster the inspiration he needs: "Suddenly a new burst of energy has occurred." In the film, this is what fires him up for the ultimate rap battle. Here, however, he at least hatches in his mind an alternative ending as he takes flight from 8 Mile, "free as a bird", leaving only a "blur" in his wake.

RAP GAME

Eminem joins up with D12 and 50 Cent on another track the pantherish musical menace and understated ambience of which are tribute to the keyboards and programming of Luis Resto. Bizarre of D12 kicks off by describing rap as the "hardest 9 to 5 you'll ever have", an unexpected assessment of hip hop's working hours, before later humorously suggesting that a debate between himself and the rest of the D12 posse as to who was the best rapper resulted in the bloody deaths of his erstwhile compadres.

Swifty asserts that rap battles of the kind Rabbit partakes in might not be for him since he's liable to "lose it" if MCs are "rude" to him and snap their necks with his bare hands, while 50 Cent brags about "making millions look easy" with an effortless style at the mic which probably accounts for his subsequent huge success. Finally, Eminem weighs in with a slapdown of C Dolores Tucker, a Washington-based, African-American campaigner who had recently turned her fire on Eminem. She had dedicated her working life to touring and lecturing on how, in her words, hip hop "denigrates and demoralizes young girls and women, and glorifies drugs, gang rape, criminal behaviour and death for young boys... the music is race-driven, greed-driven, and drug-driven. Our kids are growing up to emulate the gangster image."

After Tupac Shakur had name-checked her disparagingly, she attempted to sue the late rapper, claiming that his offensive remarks had ruined her sex life. Eminem was clearly undeterred by either this, or any racial issues involved in attacking such a proud and pre-eminent African-American female. "Tell that C Dolores Tucker slut to suck my dick," he raps.

RABBIT RUN

Now here's Rabbit in his darkest hour, on the eve of the rap battle, stoked up with domestic tribulations. Here Eminem chooses to attribute these solely to Rabbit's mom, although she's just one of a number of factors in the movie. She's finally brought him to boiling point and now his pen feels like it's bubbling over with creativity. "Goosebumps, yeah I'm going to make your hair sit up," he vows. Only not quite. In the mid-section of this chorus-less, sustained rant,

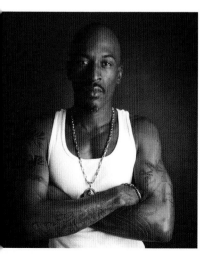

RAP LEGEND RAKIM
ALSO MAKES AN
APPEARANCE ON THE
8-MILE SOUNDTRACK.

delivered to the heavy weather of a mock-orchestral accompaniment, Eminem again departs from rap's usual subject matter. He treats us to a bout of writer's block, "Stuck in this slump," scribbling an idea, crossing it out, tearing the paper from a pad and screwing it into a ball. This is an extreme example of how much Eminem's work is about his work, as the very tortuous steps that lead to its creation is the actual subject matter.

Again, doubts come crawling back to suck him back in. "I'm afraid, why am I afraid, why am I slave to his trade," he says, but his worst moments bring out the best in him. And now he's bringing them on, rehearsing the rap battle to come in his mind, facing down his "bitch" of an opponent as the coin is flipped to see who goes up first. Now he's raring,

imagining the fear in the rival MCs' eyes as if he's Jaws coming at them, all the time massaging his own self-confidence, priming himself for action. Still, he has a deadline to meet, the clock's ticking. But he's on a roll now. "I'm a-make them eat this watch," he spits. He's absolutely ready, like a boxer who needs to be held back by his seconds, until the song ends abruptly with the dong of a bell, as if it's the beginning of round one.

What's great about "Rabbit Run" is, once again, Eminem's ability to give us a tour of his state of rap mind; a tour in which no rooms, no closets of self-doubt or embarrassment, are out of bounds. This isn't pure braggadocio but a convincing account of someone going through the psychological process of fighting off all their fears and demons.

STIMULATE

This track appears on the bonus CD that comes with the special edition of the *8 Mile* soundtrack, a sampler featuring acts from Em's label, Shady Records. Eminem's own contribution catches him in a relatively genial mood, as if mellowed out through some serious pot, something that is supported by the mock-psychedelic effects – the backward vocals, the heady swirl of guitars rising like smoke-rings from a big, fat spliff.

There's none of his usual edgy, high-metabolic, paranoid nihilism here. Without conceding ground to his opponents he comes on as reassuring and at ease with himself, even quoting Robbie Williams; "Let Me Entertain You". Chill out, he advises, trying to take the heat out of things rather than stoke it up: "My music can be slightly amusin'/You shouldn't take lyrics so seriously it might be confusin'." It's as if he's past arguing and is on the point of entering a more considered phase. "I came to uplift, let your woes begone," he assures us, adding that he "don't mean nobody harm." Older but wiser, he tut-tuts wryly as he reflects on his fans. "I try to stimulate but kids emulate," he chides (so much for the "army marching back of me"). Quit your cloning, he advises. Falling prey to the sanguine spiritualism that occasionally overcomes him when contemplating his fans, he quotes R Kelly: "I believe you can fly." Whether this was a newer, mellower Eminem talking, or just the dope, is a question that will undoubtedly be answered with his next album.

ENCORE

Following 2002's *The Eminem Show*, there was a feeling that Em had settled all accounts, both personally and artistically. He'd created a body of work which revealed all facets of his character – the hilariously evil Slim Shady, the troubled reality of the autobiographical Mathers, and Eminem, the showbiz entity in which it all, very publicly came together. The unholy trinity. It was a triumphantly complete oeuvre, in which he'd achieved vindication through fame, fortune and adulation for the poor piece of trailer trash nobody wanted to befriend, and spit in the eye of all those who would have done him down. Considered a pariah by many even as he rose to prominence, he'd found himself shortlisted by *Time* magazine for 2002's Man Of The Year. He was highly regarded not as some upstart, Caucasian brat but as an authentic cultural icon, taken seriously by commentators like Greil Marcus and Robert Christgau.

However, the very completeness of his triumph left him in a quandary – what next, for the rapper who had thrived on the continuing turbulence and adversity of his private life for his source material? What next for the artist who had nothing left to fight for, whose place in the cultural firmament was sealed? What had he left to do, what seam would he mine now? Having cleaned out his closet, it was now empty. By 2003, Eminem was at a potential career hiatus, a crossroads.

Sure, there was still friction, turbulence and conflict in Eminemworld. Ex-wife Kim, having drawn the strangest hand of any pop superstar spouse in history, was not having the best time of her life. She was, according to her lawyer, "under emotional as well as personal stress". In November 2003, according to the *Detroit Free Press*, she appeared in two Macomb County courts on bench warrants having had two earlier court hearings.

Judge Edward Servitto ordered her to be placed on an electronic tether and to undergo drug and alcohol testing and attend weekly Alcoholics Anonymous and Narcotics Anonymous meetings. She would also face a hearing on cocaine possession charges, as well as a separate charge of running a drug house, stemming from a hotel party she'd held in September. If Eminem wanted to carry on taking pops, if he still had the heart to, there, down there, was Kim.

Meanwhile, Eminem was embroiled in a series of continuing feuds, including with Ray "Benzino" Scott, whose magazine *The Source*, the one he secretly co-owned, had always had it in for Eminem. Then there was Ja Rule, with whom Eminem and protege 50 Cent's beef went back some years, although in both cases you got the feeling that maintaining hostile dialogue with such minuscule "rivals" was beneath someone of Eminem's current stature. More disturbingly, a tape had emerged (via the helpful officers of *The Source*, predictably) of the 16-year-old Eminem apparently making racist remarks in a rap, which potentially provided grist and further resentment to those who felt that no white boy deserved so much attention working in an African-American medium.

At some subconscious level at this stage in his career, you sense Eminem casting around not so much for new worlds to conquer (his excellent performance in *8 Mile* could have led to his making a Justin Timberlake-style transition to Hollywood, had he so been inclined) but new targets to bait. Encore is peppered with mischievous sideswipes at 2004 pop's most notorious, particularly some of its younger, wholesome members, though it was the relatively senior, relatively unwholesome Michael Jackson who, pompously and ill-advisedly, rose up and took offence to both the lyrical and video content of "Just Lose It".

Less predictably, the CIA hoved officially into the fray, on the basis of a lyrical segment on Eminem's "We As Americans" (eventually released on the deluxe edition of *Encore*), which had originally been leaked onto the internet in bootleg form. They eventually concluded that national security was not in jeopardy as a result of this piece of verse and that this was not the utterance

129

of a fledgling Oswald, or likely to motivate one. Still, it did presage a significant shift in Eminem's political consciousness, motivated in particular by Bush's calamitous "crusade" in Iraq, which was well under way in 2003.

Eminem had been almost cajoled into recording *Encore* by leaks like "We As Americans". He felt "whipped" into the studio, as he later put it in his autobiography *The Way I Am*. He went down to Lou Pearlman's studio in Orlando without pre-written material and the barest wisp of a concept. As ever, Dr Dre was on co-production and beat duties, while stalwarts such as keyboardist Lui Resto was once more in tow. Eminem was pleased with his output, however, once he got going, taking instrumental tracks cooked up by Dre into a separate room where, as was his wont, he would scribble out raps like mini-mind maps, less inclined to "spit out" rhymes into the mic like his admired contemporary Jay-Z. Still, the words flowed. "Once we got going we started to fly," said Eminem.

Encore was well received overall, and with good reason – it contains some towering lyrical moments, not least "Mosh", "Like Toy Soldiers" and the brilliantly condensed autobiography of "Yellow Brick Road", while technically, both rap and production-wise, there's a general feel, even in some of the album's baser moments, of guys who have been doing this a long time and developed a hand-in-glove effortlessness and mastery of their art. That said, there were certain caveats from critics who felt that, however creatively juiced Em might have claimed to have been during the sessions, there was a lack of drive and focus to the album lyrically. Alexis Petridis, writing in the *Guardian*, felt that on some of the album Eminem came across as "bored" and "going through the motions", with Dre's production "sometimes lacking its usual, inventive spark".

He also, presciently, credited Eminem with having the insight to be his own best critic. And so it was when, in 2007 and speaking to interviewer, biographer and confidant Anthony Bozza, he remarked, "*Encore* is a good record but I don't feel like it was a great record for me. It wasn't quite up to what I feel like my personal standards are for myself. It wasn't all that I'm capable of doing. It feels a little too self-loathing to me. When I go back and listen to it… it just feels like I'm pissing and moaning about whatever. It sounds like in my head I feel like I have all these things to piss and moan about. And maybe I did, maybe I didn't, I don't know, but to actually bring that kind of shit to the forefront like that, I just don't agree with it."

As Eminem would further concede, if there was a reason for this, it would be to do with his increasing intake of drugs. For, while in an interview in *Rolling Stone* conducted around the time of *Encore* he had given the

encouraging impression of someone who had "slowed down" on his drug and booze intake, in reality, as he admitted to Bozza, it had developed into a problem, if not a catastrophe. "Even though I knew it inside, I would never let on that it was a problem. Obviously I was pretty good at hiding it because I was pretty busy. I was a functioning addict. I knew in my mind, 'I'm taking these pills just for the fuck of it now.' I was taking them and I needed more and more. When I think back on my mental state back then – 'Oh, I wrote this because of this' – I can see what I was going through. Sedative drugs like Valium and Vicodin and Ambien, they certainly put a cloud over your head. They put a dumbbell in your mood." This, for Eminem, accounted for the bouts of self-pity that occasionally blight *Encore*. However, despite its flaws, the album took its due place in rap history following its release in November 2004 – the first album to sell 10,000 digital copies in its first week, a number one seller in the US, UK and across Europe and a quadruple platinum seller in the States. Misgivings, lapses, setbacks, bring them on – The Eminem show rolled relentlessly and regardlessly on.

CURTAINS UP

With a last check of the mic, and against the drone of heavy stage machinery, Eminem takes to the stage as the crowd chant his name almost ominously, as if singing "One of us!" Then, a bullet-like impact, and . . .

EVIL DEEDS

Over an unchanging, deadpan procession of sampled strings and low-key, handclap backbeat, Eminem reaches back into his old grab bag of familiar grievances. There's a mixture of emotions; a remorse, of sorts, as in an ironic twist on Christ's words on the cross he intones, in the chorus, "Father please forgive me for I know not what I do/I just never had the chance to ever meet you." He dismisses himself as his mother's "evil seed", but then, in a series of verses in which he provides his own, sardonic echo, he indignantly retorts about how his upbringing might have been misshapen; neglected by his parents, eventually taken in by "Edna and Charles" (his father's uncle, a World War II vet, and wife,

PERFORMING AT THE 2004 MTV EUROPEAN MUSIC AWARDS.

who he later described as his "saving grace"). But they can't protect him from being bullied at school, where the chant goes up, "Debbie had a Satan spawn."

Eminem then goes on to rail against the word "predominantly", generally used in the context of black or white neighbourhoods. Feeling that falls between the easy stools of racial distribution, a white man in a supposedly black man's world, shunned by both sides, he works himself into a lather; "Why do I go through so much bullshit?" Maybe it's verses like this he had in mind when he later accused himself of self-pity and even as he's rhyming, he gives vent to an imaginary voice of retort; "Man, I'd hate to have it as bad as that Mr Mathers," but Em the plaintiff has the last word; "You don't know the half of it." Thereafter, Em bounces back and forth lyrically through time to the frustrations of his childhood with all its unfulfilled Christmasses, to his present day, when fame precludes him even from an ordinary trip to the playground with his daughter. Once he was too poor to have a normal life; now he's too rich to have one. With some feeling, Eminem complains, "this ain't how it was supposed to be/Where's the switch I can turn off an on?" and, worryingly for fans so early on in the album, hints at exhaustion with his career and of "passing the baton" to 50 Cent.

NEVER ENOUGH

Given that Nate Dogg and 50 Cent contribute routinely self-aggrandising verses, "Never Enough", clocking in at 2:40, makes for a brief rap morceau, conducted to a simple, rubbery, rolling backbeat. Again, there's cause for concern in Eminem's lyric. Yes, he's conquered all, though, he believes, there'll always be doubters out there. But it feels as if he's considering his own legacy, making concluding remarks that again hint at retirement. Yes, some may have found his verses pacy and not easy to catch the first time, such was the speed of his thinking but despite the confusion he has sown, he asks only that when he's "pushing up the daisies" he will eventually be ranked among the greats and, in the heavenly hip-hop hereafter be sitting alongside Jay-Z.

As it turned out, Eminem was, in 2011 ranked "King Of Hip-Hop" by *Rolling Stone*, beating off the likes of Jay-Z on criteria made up of a combination of sales, airplay and social media presence. As for Nate Dogg, he passed away in March of the same year. "Nate's voice in music will never be replaced," said Eminem by way of tribute. "He helped create the blueprint for West Coast hip-hop, and I was one of the lucky people who had the privilege to work with him and the honour to have him as a friend."

YELLOW BRICK ROAD

One of *Encore*'s handful of peak tracks, this, one of the most indispensible Eminem lyrics. Often accused of retreading and retreading old ground and past woes, here, for the first time, he recounts in detail his initiation into hip-hop in the late 1980s as a teenager. It's anecdotally immaculate, reeling off names and period details, over one of Dre's spikier backbeats, all winding chamber strings and bustling, hustling percussion, which Eminem matches with his always rhythmically on-point verse. Kim, inevitably, plays a bit part in the drama (they'd known each other since she was 13), as Em steals a bike to meet her – then it's over to meet Proof and Goofy Gary to hand out flyers for a talent show, at which Eminem defies doubts about his pigmentation. "I spit out a line and rhymed 'birthday' with 'first place'/And we both had the same rhymes that sound alike/ We was on the same shit, that Big Daddy Kane shit, with compound syllables sound combined".

RAPPER 50 CENT WAS 'DISCOVERED' BY EMINEM IN 2002.

Written out, those lines sound ungainly but Eminem's delivery of them is exemplary of his skills as a whole – reconciling a bundle of potentially awkward clauses, blank verses and verbal tripping points into a vocal symmetry, a formidable regularity that never misses a beat or emphasis.

Eminem then goes on to deal with the scandal of the tape circulated by his foes at *The Source*, in which he is heard to rap "Never date a black girl". As someone whose political correctness towards African-Americans was always unfailing, this was potentially wounding stuff. However, Eminem rode it out well. For a start, he didn't pretend it was phoney, or doctored, or taken out of context. Secondly, he quite reasonably observed that nearly all of us in our adolescent years say things which would at best embarrass, at worst outrage us in later years but don't have dug up and exposed to the world. Thirdly, he apologised for the tape, whose background he explains in "Yellow Brick Road". It was a reaction to a brief dalliance with a black girl who'd enjoyed his rapping but the affair had fizzled out. "It backfired - I was supposed to dump her but she dumped me for this black guy." Hence the bitterness, hence the ill-advised tape. "I've heard people say they heard the tape and it ain't that bad/But it was I singled out a whole race and for that apologise." Magnanimous stuff, but trust bad Shady to sneak in the last word. "I was wrong cause no matter what colour a girl is she's still a hoe." Bam.

LIKE TOY SOLDIERS

Retrieving and dusting down Martika's '80s hit "Toy Soldiers" from the pop attic for sample fodder, this is another keynote Eminem track, among the soberest and reflective he has ever recorded, in which you sense a maturity that comes with fatherhood and with the futility of anger and rivalry that only leads to bloodshed. He reflects on his ongoing beef with the rapper Benzino, who in 2003 had compounded his secret involvement in *The Source* (which only awarded *The Marshall Mathers LP 2* mics out of 5) by recording a diss single entitled "Pull Your Skirt Up", attacking a strawman Eminem for failing in "street cred". He alludes also to Ja Rule, who had upped the stakes in his own war of words with both Eminen and 50 Cent with "Loose Change", which included the lines "Em you claim your mother's a crack head, Kim's a known slut, so what's Hailie gonna be when she grows up?"

EMINEM AND
FELLOW D12 RAPPER
PROOF AT THE 45TH
ANNUAL GRAMMY
AWARDS.

Although Eminem tossed plenty of verbal grenades back in both his enemies' direction, with extra wit and panache for good measure, on "Like Toy Soldiers", his imagination is seized by the prospect of this diss war leading to a Biggie and Tupac-style tragedy, and that he's devoted more energy and anger to it than has been good for him. It's all gotten too Pyrrhic. "Even though the battle was won, I feel like we lost it . . .

135

I'm exhausted/And I'm so caught in it I almost feel I'm the one who caused it/This ain't what I'm in hip-hop for."

All the same, even as he's drawing himself back from the fray, his gorge rises as he recounts how he tried unsuccessfully to broker a truce with Ja Rule, and can't resist from brooding once more on his Benzino beef. Still, he's determined to be "the bigger man" and emerges as such from "Like Toy Soldiers" – bigger, brighter, broader of mind than his pitifully unworthy opponents.

MOSH

Once noticeable aspect of the war against Iraq initiated by George Bush was how few rock and pop stars were willing to pit themselves against it and the

hostility endured by those such as The Dixie Chicks who dared publically to criticise their President's actions. It may be that, being Texan and country musicians, The Dixie Chicks were more expected to toe the patriotic line and therefore were particularly vilified. As a renegade pottymouth white hip-hop brat, Eminem was less likely to be seen to salute the Stars And Stripes like a good, Toby Keith-style boy – however, equally, he was not expected to demonstrate the forthright, political consciousness he demonstrates on this, another of his finest outings.

Dre sets up a muddy, trench-like backbeat as Eminem leads his imaginary troops, his legions of disaffected fans, into a war of dissent. Unlike, say, Bob Dylan, who spent a career taking oblique flight from his supposed obligations as a leader of a countercultural protest movement, Eminem has no qualms about stepping up to the plate – it's as if it appeal to his ego as much as his relish of a high-profile challenge. "Come with me and I won't steer you wrong/Put your faith and your trust as I guide us through the fog," he exhorts in the chorus. Step by step, Eminem exhorts his army through the rain, through the desert storm, to the climactic exhortation, "They tell us no we say yea, they tell us stop we say go/Rebel with a rebel yell, raise hell we gonna let em know/ Stomp, push, shove, mush, Fuck Bush, until they bring our troops home!"

EVEN PRESIDENT GEORGE W. BUSH COULD NOT EVADE EMINEM'S IRE.

Onward he marches, past bin Laden, "this monster, this coward that we have empowered", to confront the real enemy, Bush, the distracting warmonger, very possibly motivated by impressing George Bush Snr, the once-disapproving father, finishing the job against Saddam he couldn't. But, urges Eminem, if he wants a fight, let him fight himself. "Strap him with an AK-47, let him go fight his own war/Let him impress daddy that way!"

In interviews, Eminem spoke of "my people" as the American victims of the Iraq war – young men like himself, both black and white, from the wrong side of the tracks, who fought and died disproportionately in wars devised by patricians and corporate schemers like Bush and Cheney. Eminem declared himself for Kerry but Bush carried the 2004 election – this, sadly, was one battle too big for Em to prevail in. He did at least, however, earn respect from unlikely quarters such as one-time critic Moby, who admired his anti-Bush stance. "I found myself respecting him for doing that."

PUKE

From Eminem at his best, we sadly descend to Eminem at his worst. Beginning with the unedifying sounds of vomiting into a toilet (there is something of recurring body functions motif on *Encore*). It's an anti-Kim song, in which Eminem retches up the worst of his feelings against his ex-wife, against a beat hammered out like a fist on a table for emphasis. "You make me sick to my stomach," jeers Eminem, briefly and wittily excoriating himself for having a tattoo of Kim, leaving him with no option but to find a new girlfriend of the same name, considers a more sensible, epistolary approach but then decides, screw it, she'd only screw it up and throw it away so why not lay down a track instead? "You're a fuckin' coke-head slut, I hope you fuckin' die/I hope you get to hell and Satan sticks a needle in your eye/I hate your fuckin' guts, you fuckin' slut, I hope you die." At least Em's being honest to his emotions, but this comes across like a late-night ansaphone message from a bitter ex.

MY FIRST SINGLE

Again, this is hardly one of Eminem's brightest moments – it's essentially an admission of creative defeat, of failing to come up with a killer idea, and just winging and spitting stuff for the hell of it. "Supposed to be my first single/ But I just fucked that up so/Fuck it, let's all have fun let's mingle." With Dr Dre as his wingman, whom he compares to lawyer Johnny Cochran to his OJ, Eminem feels he can get away with anything and here, he just about proves the point. With a facetiously loose backbeat and Eminem recalling the languid arrogance of a Schoolly D, "My First Single" best seen as a satirical abuse of airplay time from a man who's so platinum-assured of success he can cut any old shit and get it played. Em revisits old targets like Christopher Reeve, the disabled victim of the Superman curse with whom he has a morbid obsession, there's a brief namecheck for Paris Hilton and for Britney Spears and Justin Timberlake, of whom, Eminem giggles, there is unearthed video in which they're screwing. Buzzing around from silly wordplay to puerility, the fun is only clouded by a sense that Eminem has lost his direction a little.

RAIN MAN

A reference, this to the famous Dustin Hoffman movie in which he starred opposite Tom Cruise as an austic *idiot savant* who inherits a fortune. Eminem catches Hoffmann's trademark stutter in the opening, "Definitely, definitely, definitely . . . K-Mart." He then kicks in with the line he later said was the only one he had in his head when he entered the studio in Orlando – "You find me offensive? I find you offensive." As a thought, it's almost too epigrammatic to work as a starter lyric, however, and Eminem then veers off into wordplay and stream of consciousness, in which Christopher Reeve once again figures, alongside Darth Vader and Em somehow imagines himself as the man who killed Superman, the "Bad Guy", the Kryptonite. Musing further on lesbianism, consulting Dr Dre on the protocol of sexuality, it's hard to see where Eminem is going with all of this stuff, which Eminem proceeds through to the rhythmical gait of a boy doing a silly zombie walk. In the end, the conclusion to this tour around the workings of Eminem's mid is self-deprecating. This is all he knows how to do. In his autobiography *The Way I Am*, he claims to be incapable of finding his way about by car, "clueless about directions", but ask him to navigate through a rhyme and he's as extraordinarily capable as a savant counting spilt cocktail sticks.

BIG WEENIE

This feels like a skit inflated into a full-length song with a ponderous backbeat, with Eminem playing both patient and bullying psychiatrist, a mock self-examination of why the rapper comes out with such awful, scatalogical and outrageous things, in which the examination is seen to bounce back on the inquisitor – penis size and Eminem envy are at the root of the naysayers' indignation, though with Eminem in multiple Muppet-style voice mode, it could easily be a form of self-deprecation. A raspberry-blowing piece of filler this, which again raises the question of Eminem's commitment levels. You can only hope they had a good time making this.

JUST LOSE IT

"That's not a stab at Michael," says Eminem at one point here, firmly in Shady mode, but watching the video, no one's fooled. Admittedly, it's a parade of parodies – Madonna in her pointy bra phase and MC Hammer are lampooned, in some rather outdated mickeytaking for 2004. Paris Hilton crops up briefly, rebuffing a drunken Eminem with a gutpunch. "Beer goggles" misted up, Em then accidentally makes a play for Dr Dre. He also disinters the memory of Pee Wee Herman aka Paul Reubens, whose career as a both an adult and child entertainer came to a temporary, abrupt halt when he was arrested in 1991 for masturbating in a public cinema. But it's clear that the main butt is Michael Jackson, from the squeaky, facetiously plastic funk backbeat to the frequent references to child molestation. We see Eminem as Jacko in white socks dancing in an alleyway, with his hair on fire, while the video concludes with his nose falling off and his nursing his face on the end of his bed as young children bounce up and down on it.

MICHAEL JACKSON,
ONE OF MANY
STARS PARODIED BY
EMINEM.

Meanwhile, Slim Shady plays the role of childcatcher; "Little boy – I mean, girl, touch my body." Puerile and obvious it might all seem but Jackson took it seriously enough to issue a statement of protest. "I am very angry at Eminem's depiction of me in his video," Jackson said, announcing a lawsuit. "I feel that it is outrageous and disrespectful. It is one thing to spoof, but it is another to be demeaning and insensitive. I've admired Eminem as an artist, and was shocked by this. The video was inappropriate and disrespectful to me, my children, my family and the community at large." The video would prove no distraction among the community at large from the molestation charges

Jackson faced at this time; for all his pieties, his dubious attitude towards children rather contrasts with Eminem's own; being a parent brought out all that was most wholesome, even hokum in him. Ironically, in 2007, Jackson would come to own the rights to portions of Eminem's catalogue when his Sony/ATV Music Publishing companys purchased Famous Music LLC from Viacom.

ASS LIKE THAT

Deplore the mock-Arabic voice in which Eminem conducts this infantile paean to the rear end, in which the critical term "bottom feeder" takes on new meaning, feel the despair of those highbrows who attempt to give Eminem his due as a pop figure of our time worthy of deep cultural consideration when he comes out with this as a single, shudder with every "Der doing doing doing" chorus line. Still, it can at least be said that no one but Eminem could pull off a piece as brazenly lowbrow as this and survive with his integrity intact. Some of the energy of "Just Lose It" carries over as he pants over former child stars Jessica Simpson and the Olsen singers coming of age and making the transition into sexual icons. Eminem at least has the bad taste to make sure that this phenomenon doesn't go unobserved by the wider, sexually squeamish culture; he's calling it like it is.

DETROIT-BORN RAPPER OBIE TRICE.

SPEND SOME TIME

A joint outing this, in which Eminem, Obie Trice, Stat Quo and 50 Cent get together for what's ostensibly a misogynistic grumble fest; or, as Em puts it in the intro, "If there's any bitches in this room, then there's something I gotta say." Off a spare, slow-moving backbeat, Eminem's own verse concerns a woman with whom he was so taken he almost made the mistake of introducing her to the truly sacred females in his life, his daughters. The intruder into Eminem's life should have understood that he only wanted her for "a few booty calls", and picked up on the implied message that "When we fucked I refused to even take my jewellery off." The verse does explore more complex feelings, as Eminem admits to being more drawn to the girl the more she gets broody and argues. It's redeemed by his honesty about his emotional confusion.

MOCKINGBIRD

Over the gentle patter of a hip-hop rendition of the famous lullaby, Eminem addresses his two daughters and gives the belching, the leching and the disaffection and rage to one side as he gives vent to his most dominant emotion – his desire to protect his children, to keep them from all the lovelessness, the insanity and deprivation that have blighted his own life. He can't, of course, pretend that all's fine between their Mommy and Daddy; "I can see it in your eyes, deep down you wanna cry."

Kim had certainly had her problems, and Eminem found himself in the position of having to shield his daughters from her personal difficulties with the law. "In the last year, Kim has been in and out of jail and on house arrest, cut her tether off, had been on the run from the cops for quite a while," Em told *Rolling Stone* in 2004. "Trying to explain that to my niece and my daughter was one of the hardest things I ever had to go through. You can never let a child feel like it's her fault for what's goin' on. You just gotta let her know: 'Mom has a problem, she's sick, and it's not because she doesn't love you. She loves you, but she's sick right now, and until she gets better, you've got Daddy. And I'm here.'"

Conversely and poignantly, he lyrically recalls the early days when Kim had to carry the can for him, alone and terrified in a frequently burgled house while Em was trying to get his rap career going. He remembers Kim putting Christmas presents under the tree for Hailie and saying they were from Daddy "'cause Daddy couldn't buy them". The pain of that Christmas acted as a spur to Eminem to be a provider. Perhaps thankfully, the sentimental mood of the song doesn't hold out; in the pay-off line; "And if that mockingbird don't sing . . . I'm a break that birdie's neck," before signing off, with a malicious cackle.

CRAZY IN LOVE

"You're the ink to my paper . . .The moral, the very fibre/The whole substance to my rap /You are my reason for being/The meaning of my existence /If it wasn't for you/I would never be able to spit this." Musically, there's not much going on in "Crazy In Love" - it kicks in with a squealing, sped-up, shrunken sample of Heart's "Crazy On You", before tracking Eminem's rhyming with some workaday Dre beats. However, especially following the likes of "Puke", this is the most comprehensively honest assessment of Eminem towards Kim, even if it involves the words "fuckin' bitch" and allusion to some, hopefully, lyrically imaginary domestic violence against her. It's not exactly "Wind Beneath My Wings", nor exactly a loving tribute but it does touch extensively on Em's compulsive, addictive attachment to Kim and also that she is somehow his creative support system, even if her role as one is as an object of abuse and vented, twisted frustration. He also grudgingly acknowledges her tacitness; "You never step out of line." Truly, Kim is the oddest and most put-upon of muses. If only we could hear more from her.

ONE SHOT 2 SHOT

One thing that can be said for Eminem is that, unlike many of his superstar peers, the cast of his supporting characters has always remained pretty constant. Here, he gives an outing to members his D12 posse. There's a shootout at a nightclub, conveyed in flashback/flashforward narrative, conducted to caps popping over a stalking, almost jaunty reggae piano lilt. Rather ungallantly, Em uses as a human shield a girl who had dissed him earlier but is now tearfully apologetic; she gets hit, he dumps her to make his escape to go fetch his .38, regroup his posse and eventually turn the tables. It's a chance to namecheck the various D12 members, and to boast that their gigs are so rammed that they require the attention of the fire marshal, though it's arguable that without Eminem's patronage, they might well not have advanced so far.

ENCORE/CURTAINS DOWN

Continuing the dual themes of firearms and male camaraderie, "Encore" sees Eminem gather in and throw arms around the shoulders of his compadres Dr Dre and 50 Cent, in what's essentially a celebration of three hip-hop guys at the top of their game, at *the* top of the game, three against the world, on top of the world. To a distant, barking backbeat, abrasive spasms of sampled guitar, and some parodic hints of "Jump" by House Of Pain (whose Everlast was another nemesis of Enimem). They're entitled to swagger. "Enough with all the pissin' and moanin', whinin' and bitchin'," barks Eminem. "Sit and observe, listen, you'll learn if you pay attention/Why ten multi-platinum albums later, three diamond/World-wide, we're on the charts with a bullet and still climbin'". But there's an ominous air of finality about the chorus. "And if they don't let us in through the front/We'll come through the side/'Cos I don't ever wanna leave the game without/At least saying goodbye/So all my people on the left, all my people on the right/Swing one last time." This is the strongest hint yet that Eminem was looking to make a final bow, having said and done it all. However, as the track kicks into "Curtains Down", Eminem produces a piece and a final surprise; he's taking his audience with him. Rapid gunfire, multiple screams, then a robotic "see you in hell." A vengeance fantasy not on his fans but on the absurdity of showbiz adulation.

WE AS AMERICANS

Thanks in part to some Latin tinges from longtime keyboardist Luis Resto, this beat rolls as slickly as any produced by or for Eminem during this period. He's on good form on the mic too, particularly when he drifts off point in this verbose variation on the old "Fuck The Police" anti-stop and search theme, demonstrating his instinctive grasp of rap phonetics and unorthodox meter, even as he's spitting bullets of abuse; "You wanna harass with this limo tinted glass/flashing this flashlight on my ass where was you at/last night when them assholes/ran up on my glass … kiss the crack on my cracker slashed ass."

However, there was a brief frisson as a result of an almost throwaway couplet in which Eminem vigorously protested his anti-mercenary approach to his craft. "Fuck money I don't rap for dead Presidents/I'd rather see the

President dead." The "Dead Presidents" reference is clearly to dollar bills, the second line Eminem's way of saying "I swear on my life this is the truth." Initial reports suggested that the Secret Service would be looking into the lyric, as confirmed by official spokesperson John Gill. However, it just as quickly emerged that this was a routine matter, given the nature of the lyric and they had routinely decided Eminem presented no threat, very possibly after an enquiry that lasted less than 60 seconds. Eminem was later allegedly to prove himself useful to the CIA. A human rights watch group claimed that inmates in Afghanistan were forced to listen to his music for up to 20 days while detained in pitch black cells.

LOVE YOU MORE

Another fine addition to the Deluxe addition of the album; commencing with another of Eminem's fantasy shooting scenarios, the backbeat combines a resigned layer of piano with Bach-in-the-cigar-ad-style melancholic resignation with the machine gun patter of electric percussion. It's another song in which Eminem wrestles with his contradictory, sado-masochistic relationship with Kim. "The more you put me through/The more it makes me want to come back to you," he intones, again and gain in the chorus, with his anger mounting methodically with each line and verse, redder and rawer, a la "Stan" or "The Way I Am". "Cos' we truly love each other, that's why we always fight/And all we do is shove each other every other fuckin' night/And it's clear, it ain't gonna change, this pinned up rage." This is a subject Eminem returns to repeatedly; had he left it at this one track, it would have been ample.

RICKY TICKY TOC

Another stylish backbeat, this, a Jew's harp-style riff lending a faintly Spaghetti Western tint to proceedings. "I'm ready to go so bad, I'm going bananas," claims Em, raring to go, in what amounts to a tribute to his own good fortune in teaming up with Dre and then later 50 Cent, like hitting the jackpot and winning the lottery in the same lifetime. "Maxell Cassettes" get a namecheck, an almost quaint allusion to just how long Em had been in the game – only a few years less than hip-hop itself had been around. A nice concluding touch, too, as the track judders to a crashing halt on the line, "And you don't stop."

AN OUTRAGEOUS PERFORMANCE AT THE 2005 MTV MOVIE AWARDS.

145

RELAPSE

It's not often in pop or rock music that artists step back, the way sportspeople are obliged to when age catches up with them, and accept that they have contributed all they have to. Usually, retirement is forced on them, or, if it isn't, they willingly accept the invitation to play on by public, if not critical demand. Kraftwerk effectively ceased in 1986, once their project of electrifying the pop landscape was complete. Elvis sat out much of the 60s, which, for whatever reason, was just as well. After *Encore*, and as strongly hinted, Eminem was apparently set to join the small band of voluntary retirees. He appeared to have accepted, serenely, that with 75 million albums sold there was little left for him to say or prove and looked set to step up into a more executive role, like a footballer going into management, with 50 Cent his star player. "I felt like I had to pull back from the spotlight," he later said. "I thought I'd try to produce records and work with artists from my label and shit like that. I thought this would be my way to pull back a little bit and not be the front man."

From a distance, once could imagine Eminem with his feet up and the world as his footstool, not even in his mid-30s but able to bask in his conquests, let younger, hungrier men take the strain on the mic as he cast himself in the role of producer, mentor and occasional guest. Following *Encore* he put out a greatest hits album, July 2005's *Curtain Call: The Hits*, and in 2006 presented *The Re-Up*, showcasing the posse on his own Shady Records label.

The truth was, however, the Eminem had not let it go; he'd temporarily lost it. "I never stopped working," he later told Anthony Bozza of that period, "but I had a problem I was hiding. I guess it was a combination of writer's block and being

RIGHT: DESHAUN HOLTON AKA 'PROOF'.

lazy, because I just didn't want to write rhymes any more." It turned out he and Dre had gone down to the studio and tried to lay down tunes but emerged with nothing.

At the heart of the problem was Eminem's addiction to painkillers, which had only escalated during and after the *Encore* sessions. He cancelled the European leg of his Anger Management Tour in 2005 and announced he was entering rehab. He gained weight. He lapsed into depression. Bizarrely, in January 2006, he even remarried Kim, as if for something to do, only to divorce her three months later, filing on April 15. The more closely you examine Eminem at this time, the more you sense him bound by old loyalties, by inescapable realities, in which the word "trappings", as applied to fame and fortune, was unfortunately apposite.

All of which was exacerbated on April 11, 2006 when his best friend and earlier mentor, DeShaun Holton, aka Proof of D12, was shot to death after an altercation with a veteran, one Keith Bender Jr following a pool game in a seedy Detroit bar, in which Bender was also killed, supposedly by Proof. A bouncer, Mario Etheridge, was found to have acted in lawful defence of another man in shooting Proof; but the precise circumstances of the tragedy were later disputed. Whatever, Proof was dead, and this only sent Eminem into a further descent. "I went through a

lot when he died. It was the worst time in my life. It just gave me a real legitimate excuse, in my head at least, to use drugs. I didn't care if my drug problem got worse at that point so I took more pills. And the more I said fuck it and took more pills, the higher my tolerance got. It's a vicious cycle."

Only in 2008 did he begin to emerge from what he had termed his "limbo" in a call to a New York radio station during an interview with 50 Cent. The lowest point came in December 2007 when he was admitted to hospital following a Methadone overdose that caused him to collapse on his bathroom floor. Finally, Em managed to haul himself out of the pit of addiction, but not without help from what at one time would have seemed a most improbable source. To the rescue, Elton John, once the subject of Em's homophobic derision, now a mentor. "(Elton) had a substance-abuse problem in the past. So when I first wanted to get sober, I called him, because he's somebody in the business who can relate to the lifestyle and how hectic things can be," Eminem told a Detroit newspaper. "He understands, like, the pressure and any other reasons that you wanna come up with for doing drugs."

EMINEM AND ELTON JOHN END THEIR DUET AT THE 43RD ANNUAL GRAMMY AWARDS.

Finally, Eminem mustered the courage to return to the studio, to begin the on-off recording process that would eventually yield *Relapse* in 2009. Initially, in order to get round his writer's block, Em, encouraged by producer Jeff Bass, would begin by adopted the Jay-Z approach of "spitting" or freestyling into the mic rather than use prepared material. Eventually, Em would relinquish Bass's services and Dre would take over production duties as recording moved to the Effigy Studios in Michigan and they would fall back into their familiar working patterns, Dre supplying the beats for Em to riff off verbally.

The breakthrough for Eminem came following a conversation with Dre. Em felt that, what with media scrutiny on what he intended to do next that he was under pressure to reinvent himself – hence, his writers' block. However, as Dre pointed out to him, bluntly and repeatedly. "Man, people want to see you, they just want to hear you get the fuck out there again." Eventually, it clicked with Eminem. He didn't need to mutate or mature into some other form of rap animal; he needed to rediscover the old Eminem, the one the public had taken to in the first place. Hence, the

"Relapse" of the title isn't a reference to drugs, but to the incorrigible Eminem doing what he always did best – being his good old, bad boy can't help it, self. "I was trying to create a triple entendre with the [album] title: relapsing literally, going back to the old days." he said. From this point on, the beats and rhymes flowed, but fuelled by sobriety rather than dulled by substances.

EMINEM ACCEPTS AN AWARD FROM ELTON JOHN AT THE 2001 BRIT AWARDS.

Not all critics approved of the New Eminem/ Same As The Old Eminem. However, although

Relapse is spotted with Eminem's bratty preoccupations, with the spirit of Slim Shady rampant, his extraordinary candour and willingness to put his life on the lyrical line once again lift *Relapse* above the rap norm. After four Eminem-less years, and a tight lid kept on internet leaks, sheer ravenous curiosity propelled the album to number one all over the world; in the USA it was the top selling hip-hop album of the year and reached double platinum status in 2010.

3AM

Following an opening skit in which Wire co-star Dominic West plays a drugs counsellor whose advice backfires on Eminem, he launches into this slasher fantasy, to a stalking, low budget soundtrack. Reality and fantasy intertwine – Eminem on the pills, channel surfing, ogling over Hannah Montana in a slough of apathy. But in the fantasy context of rap, he's able to convert his woes into bodycounts; his relapse has terrible, exterior consequences for wider society, as he blacks out and goes on a serial killing spree, waking up at McDonalds covered in blood. He mock-reminisces, like a latter-day Peter Kurten, about past murders, and discusses his bloodlust offhandedly, in a slightly strained, cod-Jamaican accent. In reality, Eminem's preoccupation with serial killing did not transcend the cinema variety. Watching these films was a deliberately retrograde step, to get him back into an old-style, dark and nasty Eminem mindset.

CURTIS '50 CENT' JACKSON.

"I found that going back through my DVD collection and watching movies about killers sparked something in me," he said, of this song. "The way a serial killer's mind works, just the psychology of them, is pretty fucking crazy. But most of that imagery came from my own mind. I did everything I could to relapse into the old me. When you relapse you go into your old ways harder than before.

In that song I relapse in a rehab facility or something like it. I just black out and fucking kill everybody. – just blacking the fuck out and killing everyone."

There's some great wordplay here, some skilled work on the mic, particularly on the "coroner/corner/cornea sequence in the opening verse.

MY MOM

With its brassy riff, and the mock-sing-song tone in which he intones the chorus; ("My mom love Valium and lots of drugs, That why I am like I am cause I'm like her") and his tendency to fly off into fantasy at a line's notice, it's hard to verify just how seriously to take the central accusation of "My Mom", which is, in essence, that in order to pacify her hyperactive little boy, she mixed valium into his food. But there's a feeling of great authenticity about the way he recounts the memories, reliving their vicious exchanges at the table which rings uncomfortably true, even if it's doubtful she would have been so candid about what she was up to as she is in these verses.

There's a lot of anger in the song; but also a strange sense of resignation to the inevitable, Larkin-esque fucking-up process perpetrated by parents (including his absent father) on offspring. Perhaps that accounts for the almost matter-of-fact neutrality with which he delivers the chorus line. Yeah, it was down to her being a drug addict also, but what are you gonna do? He even apologises for revisiting the subject of his mother. At one point, he says "All right, Ma, you win" in a sort of reverse-Cagney lyrics move. Made it to the bottom of the world. In the outtro, he cackles, perhaps sarcastically, or perhaps not, "Haha, sorry Mom, still love you though." and delivers a noisy kiss to her from afar, wherever she is, in her deteriorated state, detached from her son.

INSANE

Eminem stated that his intention with this song was to "disgust" the listener and "make them puke" but the reaction it provokes is more disconcerting. It sees him burst into chainsaw-wielding Shady mode, perform a striptease and play ping-pong with his own body parts – but the real business of the song is an accusation that his stepfather sexually abused him. "Marshall, I just love you boy, I care about your well being/ No Dad, I said no, I don't need no help peeing!" Even if this is a case of Slim Shady crying wolf, it's disquietingly vivid stuff, that feels like it has some relationship to some sort of truth. Em's opening gambit, that he was "born with a dick in my brain, yeah fucked in the head", along with the "skeletons in his closet" is doubtless in reference to his two Uncles, Todd and Ronnie Nelson, both of whom committed suicide, carriers of the bad mental seed in the Eminem ancestry.

Musically, "Insane" feels like it's about to burst into The Specials' "Ghost Town". It also contains interpolations from "Jock Box" by The Skinny Boys, who were themselves '80s hip-hop ancestors to Shady/Eminem on the vicious likes of "Rip The Cut" ("I'm like the mainman Hitler").

BAGPIPES FROM BAGHDAD

Or to put it another way, Eminem's special tribute to Mariah Carey, with whom he claimed to have had a brief fling, though Carey herself curtly downplayed any talk of an affair. "I knew him, kind of vaguely, eight years ago, on a purely platonic level, and then he wasn't my friend any more and I was like, OK, whatever," said Carey, dismissively, in a *Guardian* interview in 2009, taking umbrage at what she saw as his bizarrely unwarranted lyrical put-downs and responding with her own single, "Obsessed", about a desperate, would-be hip-hopper, stalker dude. She also threatened to set her new husband Nick Cannon, a boxing enthusiast, on Eminem, who in this song goads the pair of them relentlessly.

MARIAH CAREY, UNWILLING SUBJECT OF EM'S LYRICS

Certainly, delivered over the snakcharmer strains of a pungi flute and delivered in the sort of silly, garbled, multi-ethnic tones that indicate Eminem is in latterday Shady mode, "Bagpipes From Baghdad" is riotously, ridiculously offensive, before you even get to the verse about lesbian vegetables. His message to Mariah is clear; he would consider it an honour if she would consider stepping out with him, her current relationship status notwithstanding. Or, as Em puts it, And yeah baby, I want another crack at ya/You can beat me with any spatula thatcha want."

In case anyone's minded to take all this entirely seriously, Em offers his own, affectedly shocked critique at the unexpurgated contents of his own head in the chorus. "When will it ever cease, for Pete's sake he's crazy, to say the least … What's goin' through my mind half the time, when I rhyme?"

HELLO

Not, unsurprisingly, a cover of the Lionel Ritchie song but a Slim Shady outing. Only, Slim seems kind of jaded, and without the energy for his usual evil sexual skullduggery. Eminem spoke of being so enervated by drugs at this point in his life that he could barely rouse himself to masturbate and here, Shady is similarly afflicted with ennui. Having initially threatened to put the neck of a girl he spots in the gym in his mouth, he finds himself digressing, rapping about lithium, Jack Daniels and the fact that he doesn't even need to buy his own drugs any more because "people give me 'em."

He tries his chat-up lines; "The way your titties are wiggling and your booty shakin like Jello/Girl I don't mean any harm all I wanted to do is just say Hello." This would be slap-in-the-face stuff for most mortals but for Slim Shady it amounts to half-hearted reticence. He even turns down a female because it would involve unprotected sex and "disease is something I'm trying to keep my penis free from."

SAME SONG AND DANCE

To a smooth, worming, sleazy riff, Eminem here corrals the superstar names of the day for abduction fantasies. First up is Lindsay Lohan, whose career on *Nickelodeon* and in and out of rehab he recaps before enticing her into his car; "Slowly she gets in and I begin to lynch her/With 66 inches of extension cord." Next up is old favourite Britney Spears; again, no prizes for guessing her identity. "She twirls and turns and flirts in skirts so bad it hurts/It irked me and made me mad at first . . .but what was really going on/Was that I had developed a crush," admits Em. "Should I cut off one of my ears and mail it to her? Send her... footage of me impaling myself on an elephant tusk?" Of course, Eminem can't leave it here and completes his subjugation in the chorus. "Girl shake that ass/You ain't ever gonna break that glass/The windshield's too strong for you/I said yeah baby, sing that song/It's the last song you'll ever get the chance to sing." Eminem, always civil and reasonable in interviews, insisted that lyrics like these were never to be taken personally by the celebrities; they're merely to be taken as him trepanning his skull for twisted, cartoon lyrical content. By this stage, however, it's hard to get up any sort of response to this sort of many-times-refried outrage, beyond a modicum of technical admiration for Em's advanced rapology.

WE MADE YOU

The first single from Relapse was a precursor to the album, accompanied by a video in featuring the usual cavalcade of celebrity lookalikes and high jinks, with Eminem himself, whose own coolness is generally the first thing to be thrown on the bonfire of the vanities, playing a rather nerdy Mr Spock on a recreated Star Trek bridge. Over a backbeat that combines a sashaying, Bugsy Malone sensibility with samples of Walter Egan's "Hot Summer Nights", and a slight return of the flatulence which was such a malodorous feature of Encore, Eminem sets the tone of the forthcoming album, with a lyrical cocktail of Jessica Simpson-baiting, drug allusions and cartoon hot lesbian action.

However, there are two significant additions to Eminem's cavalcade of female butts; Amy Winehouse, then making a name for herself as much for her substance and boyfriend abuse problems as for her music, and Sarah Palin, who was doubtless stirring in Eminem the same feelings of ambivalence as she did in the minds and loins of many lusty Republican-haters, following her emergence onto the political scene. "Give me my Ventolin inhaler and two Xenadrine/And I'll invite Sarah Palin out to dinner then nail her."

MEDICINE BALL

One of the better production jobs on *Relapse*, this; imagine Godzilla destroying a Legoland Manhattan. It finds Eminem in typically attention-seeking, gross mode; after limbering up with some home abortion; ("Dig her foetus out with a wire hanger then digest her"), Eminem then turns his attention, once more to his prolonged fixation on Christopher Reeve, already five years dead at this point. Still, Em sounds indignant that he should be reproved for his continuing lampooning of the ill-fated Superman actor, whom, he insists, merely happens to be lyrically convenient. "Now everybody's pissed at me like it's my fault his name rhymes with so many different words." He sportingly allows Reeve the last word, however, issuing a challenge to the chuckling Em from beyond the grave; "Throw down the cardboard/Let's break dance if you think your hardcore."

STAY WIDE AWAKE

Retrospectively, Eminem said it was only by the time he came to record this, one of the later tracks he laid down, that he felt he'd really worked the drugs out of his system. Over a spectral riff, as befits a rapper who compares himself to the "ghost of Mozart", it's another of his explorations of the serial rapist/killer mindset, whose extremes he at once relishes and feels artistically obliged to explore in full and therefore test the sensibilities of his listeners. "There's a monster inside of me it's quite ugly and it frightens me," Em confesses. Anyway, here it's the turn of a girl called Brenda, accosted (in typically gory detail) in a wintry Central Park in the dark.

OLD TIME'S SAKE

Despite his vast audience, it often seems that Eminem in recording mode is engaged in an exclusive conversation with Dr Dre; they only have ears for each other. That certainly feels to be the case on this mutually celebratory track, in which they big up their skills, with Dre raising a "Henny and coke" as, from several million feet in the air, Eminem urinates on the girls and evades the clutches of CSI. That West Indian accent, still a little mangled, is in evidence again but there's a pure phonetic pleasure, in syllables for their own sake, in lines like; "Baby, make us some French toast and show us some skin/I show you every inch grows of my foreskin/Show me nipple I pinch, throw up, and throw up a ten/Now you know it's a sin to tease, blow us again."

ANOTHER TRIUMPH AT THE 2009 MTV VIDEO MUSIC AWARDS.

MUST BE THE GANJA

Never mind gangsta – this is ganja rap, pure and intoxicating. There's no *Thoughts Of Mary Jane* with Eminem, no *Lucy In The Sky With Diamonds*; he's upfront and to the point, in what is, despite his good rehab intentions, as close a sonic simulation of the fuzzy, illicitly pleasurable sensation of being high as hip-hop has achieved, thanks not least to the looping, amber glow of Dre's production. "This is neither the time nor the place to get macho/ So crack a six pack, sit back with some nachos/Maybe some popcorn, watch the show and just rock slow," recommends an almost aggressively mellow Eminem. But in the midst of the haze and the hedonism, the bragging and the wordplay, he's sharp, his vocals taking an angular, sober turn as he riffs with almost autistic relentlessness on his serial killer fixation. "Who ever existed in a row, put them in chronological order/Beginning with Jack the Ripper/ Name the time and place from the body, the bag, the zipper/Location of the woods where the body was dragged and then dumped/The trunk that they was stuffed in, the model, the make, the plate?"

DEJA VU

Following the "Mr Mathers" sketch, in which he revisits his Methadone OD and hospitalisation, Em delivers a rueful take on his addictions on the most lucid, sober and gratifyingly sombre moment on the album thus far. He reflects on his perpetual need to fill an empty pit in his stomach with a cycle of food, drugs and alcohol, reliving the mental patterns and desperate habits of the hopeless addict, barely able to function. The thought of his daughters staring at his bearded, apathetic face and realising something is very wrong with Daddy.

The song also contains one of what are surprisingly few allusions, at this recording stage, to the death of Proof. For an artist whose work is perpetual autobiography, you might have thought this was a subject to which he would return repeatedly and in detail; however, he merely mentions him in passing, condemning himself for using him as "an excuse" to "use". This would not have been because Em had no feelings for his friend and mentor; quite the contrary. The very first words of his autobiography *The Way I Am* are; "I can't even bring myself back to the place I was when I heard what happened to Proof. I have never felt so much pain in my life. It's a pain that is with me to this day." A pain, it seems, too deep to mine for much lyrical content.

BEAUTIFUL

A milestone, this, in that it marks Eminem's debut on production. However, for the man who remarks here, "I may be done with rap/I need a new outlet," solo production may not necessarily be his forte purely on this evidence. He chooses as his sample "Reaching Out", a rather squally, lachrymose track by post-Freddie Mercury Queen, which suits the lavishly mawkish, at times downright self-pitying tone of the lyric as a whole. While the sheer lyrical cadence of Eminem in full candid flow is a pleasure in its own right, his extended, woe-is-me spiel is rather at odds with the rest of the album's more practically humorous or pitilessly self-examining context. His lyrical touch deserts him as he resorts to clichés such as "tears of a clown" and walking a mile in another man's shoes. He takes aim at the yes-men who laugh at all his jokes, but moments of mirth are few and far between on "Beautiful".

"I think I'm starting to lose my sense of humour/Everything is so tense and gloom," he reflects, revisiting again the privations of his fatherless childhood." Having assured himself that he is "beautiful"; those who disagree can "get fucked", he metaphorically dandles his daughters on his knee and passes on the same message to them. An excusable indulgence.

CRACK A BOTTLE

"Ooww Ladies and gentlemen/The moment you've all been waiting for/In this corner. weighing 175 pounds, with a record of 17 rapes, 400 assaults, and 4 murders,the undisputed, most diabolic villain in the world: Slim Shady!" An abrupt change of mood, then, as Em kicks back in the studio with guests and old buddies 50 Cent and Dr Dre.

As with any bunch of guys together, the mood is unlikely to be soul-searching and introspective, and Eminem takes this opportunity to kick back and unleash his Shady self on another fantasy cruise for compliant females. "You just hit the lotto/Uh-oh, uh-oh, bitches hopping in my Tahoe/Got one riding shotgun and no not one of them got clothes/Now where's the rubbers? Whose got the rubbers?/I notice there's so many of them and there's really not that many of us."

There's something about the way Eminem delivers these lines – nasal and nerdy, eyes on stalks, in contrast to Dre and 50 Cent's comfier, more casual approach, that lends an "in your dreams" air to these lines, though such a lifestyle was undoubtedly at his disposal at this point. But then, perhaps his appeal is that his audience sense it's as much a fantasy for Em as it is for themselves.

The song had initially surfaced on a mixtape in 2008 and it had been thought it might feature on an upcoming 50 Cent album. Its central sample from Mike Brant's "Mais Dans La Lumière", is also used by The Wu-Tang Clan on their 2005 track "Del Tha Funkee Homosapien".

UNDERGROUND

Emerging as if silhouetted against thunderclaps and lightning flashes in a slasher movie opening, Eminem tears through these verses as if through flesh with a blade, dispatching Christopher Reeve yet again and doing unspeakable things to Hannah Montana along the way, "cut open like cantaloupe and canopy beds". Once again, Eminem equates his comeback with the reappearance of a serial killer; he may be underground, but up jerks his hand from the freshly turned soil of the grave to grab the listener by the ankles. He namechecks Jason Vorhees and Hannibal Lecter, whom he punishes by placing him in a fruit and vegetable stall, while he takes a baseball bat up Elm Street and does

VOODOO EXPERIENCE, NEW ORLEANS 2009.

battle with Freddy Krueger and even the benign Edward Scissorhands. What this all demonstrates far more tellingly than Em's Blockbuster habits is his sheer, honed, virtuosity on the mic, delivering syllables with a dazzling, threshing machine-like fluency and a sure sense of how to cut verbally what he commits to paper. All very funny, especially when he segues into a Ken Kaniff sketch, in which our anti-hero does an obscene, rasping song and dance routine at an AA meeting, clearing the hall. A perfect, anti-climactic outtro.

RECOVERY

Relapse was supposed to be followed by Relapse 2. However, on reflection, Eminem decided he needed to make another clean break, another disassociation. Much as he had reflected that *Encore* wasn't all he had hoped it would be, so he retrospectively chided himself for some of the aspects of *Relapse*. He hadn't rid himself of the drugs, the toxins in his blood, as much he liked to think he had. The conceit of renewing himself by going back to the "old" Eminem had worked, kind of, but had resulted in a little too much silliness, as signified by what he saw as his over-use of mock foreign accents. He hadn't quite been "himself".

ACTOR SACHA
BARON COHEN AS
'BRUNO' MEETS
EMINEN AT THE 2009
MTV AWARDS.

"HOME & HOME'
CONCERT AT YANKEE
STADIUM IN 2010

So, no Relapse 2; surplus material from those sessions would eventually be issued as a bonus disc. Instead, a clean break, this time for real. No skits. No accents. A lot of straight talking and a newer, sombre sense of purpose, as indicated by a fresh project title, *Recovery*, and the cover art to the album, which depicted a solitary Eminem, setting out on the open road.

This might have been Eminem's existential situation but the reality from a recorded perspective was something of a cast of thousands. Dr Dre was still in the house but so were a whole brace of other producers, who shared duties across the album, including DJ Khalil, Just Blaze and Script Shepherd. The roll call of musicians was extensive also, as well as the number of studio locations, which included Allure Sound in Oak Park, Michigan, Black Chiney Studios in Lauderdale Lakes, Florida, Boi-1da Studio in Ajax, Ontario, Canada, Playhouse in Parkland, Florida, Avex Honolulu Studio in Honolulu, Encore Studios in Burbank, California, Sun Studios in Temple Bar, London, and Shake 'Em Down Studios in New York.

For all his protestations of maverick solitude, of the world being against him, of how low he had sunk and where he had had to come from (or perhaps, precisely because of these things), by June 2010, the date of *Recovery*'s release, Eminem was, by a great many modern measurements, the world's biggest pop star. In the ensuing months he would be declared "King Of Rap". He would be the first recording artist to achieve over 40 million "likes" on Facebook. He had been showered with an almost embarrassing quantity of accolades by the Grammy authorities – winner of Best Rap Album five times, with a fresh haul of baubles in 2011. Clean and something of a fitness fanatic nowadays, the supply of controversy and friction was no longer as plentiful in his life.

Yes, there was that incident at the 2009 MTV movie awards when Sacha Baron Cohen, in the guise of his gay fashionista character Bruno, abseiled into the auditorium dressed as an angel, and landed, bare buttocks first, on Eminem, prompting the rapper to storm out in disgust. Turned out, however, that they'd planned the whole thing together. Eminem was embedded in showbiz, increasingly moderate and mainstream in his stated

opinions, steering well clear of the possibility of excess. (He toured less frequently, mindful of how easy it is to fall off the wagon when on the road). And, for all his continued Shady tomfoolery, he was even functioning as a role model, of sorts, with videos of singles from *Recovery* held up as supportive of anti-bullying and anti-domestic violence campaigns.

DAY 3 AT BONNAROO 2011, MANCHESTER, TENNESSEE.

The album was dedicated "2 anyone who's in a dark place tryin' to 2 get out. Keep your head up … It does get better!" It certainly had for Eminem. Here, he was, the biggest artist in the world, having turned every corner, his body clean, his demons banished, no longer embroiled in family problems (rumours that surfaced in 2010 that he was to return to Kim were flatly denied), those with whom he had beefs pulverised with steak hammers, enemies faded away, successful beyond anything he had even dared to imagine. *Recovery* wasn't universally well received by the critics, some of whom wondered if Eminem wasn't running on memories of past successes. But overall, the major organs such as *Rolling Stone* and *Spin* were positive. Commercially, the album reached a disappointing peak position of number 34 – in Mexico. This however, was compensated for by number one placings in Australia, Austria, Canada, Denmark, Ireland, New Zealand, the UK and the US. He was alone on the road because he was so far ahead of everyone else. And, yet there remained the nagging question, one that might breed future difficulties, bring fresh corners to turn; is this it?

COLD WIND BLOWS

Produced by Just Blaze and built around the cheap but sturdy keyboard sounds of Gringo's "Patriotic Song", this opener sees Eminem flying out of the traps, protesting perhaps a bit too much about his badass credentials, letting the profanity and insults fall where they may, citing a general sense of intense provocation against himself that's hard to put your finger on. Michael J Fox takes over the old Christopher Reeve role of physically stricken celebrity; even his supposed friend and drugs counsellor gets it. "Motherfucker might as well let my lips pucker/Like Elton John, cause I'm just a mean cocksucker/This shit is on, cause you went and pissed me off." Lines like "I'll kick a bitch in the cunt/Til it makes her queef and sounds like a fucking whoopy cushion/Who the fuck is you pushin', you musta mistook me for some sissy." are evil indeed but it's like Eminem is testing out his old capacity for lyrical meanness, checking the screw is still nice and loose in his head. It's all framed; at one point he has God strike him by lightning, and even begs forgiveness for his iniquities. "Call it evil that men do, lord forgive me for what my pen do."

TALKIN' 2 MYSELF

With a gristly, soft-metal backbeat produced by DJ Khalil, Eminem complains of feeling "all alone" in this world despite his millions of dollars and album sales and fans hanging on his every autobiographical word. But then, only Eminem can be Eminem and endure all that that entails. He demonstrates one of his best qualities on this excellent track, brute, confessional honesty. "I almost made a song dissing Lil Wayne", he confesses. "It's like I was jealous of him, cause of the attention he was getting/I felt horrible about myself, he was spitting and I wasn't/Anyone who was buzzing back then could of got it/Almost went at Kanye too, god it feels like I'm going psychotic." The track is an apology to the fans he's let down with his last two albums; "*Encore* I was on drugs, *Relapse* I was flushing 'em out/I've come to make it up to you, now no more fucking around/I got something to prove to fans cause I feel like I let 'em down." This time, he promises, he's back to full strength, and, certainly here, he pumps with the palpable energy of a man restored to maximum mental and physical fitness.

ON FIRE

Three tracks, three different producers, three different tacks. This time, it's old Detroit and D12 hand Mr Porter, with a more laid-back, arrogantly languid beat. Again, Eminem strains at the leash to impress, and impress he does with syllabically loaded lines like "Shit dissin' me is just like pissin off the Wizard of Oz/Wrap a lizard in gauze, beat you in the jaws with it." Taking the "scenic route" around the graphic byways of his sick mind, he boasts of beating up homeless vets but leaving them with nine grand, again complains of a strange feeling of aloneness, the loneliness of a man at the top of his own mountain. "Then why the fuck am I yellin' at air?/I ain't even talkin to no one, cause ain't nobody there/Nobody will fuckin' test me cause these hoes won't even dare." The track as a whole is dedicated in a foreword to critics who's occasional savagings of Eminem, he complains, are levelled without any knowledge of his personal circumstances, of where he's coming from.

WON'T BACK DOWN

"I knew vocally she'd smash it," said Eminem of Pink, who delivers a chorus here that's smashing indeed. One of the more engaging features of Recovery is his collaborations with strong female vocalists. In the past, as with Dido

or Martika, the female voices were distant, "ghostlike" samples, unaware of their future role as supplementary to Eminem's blistering raps. On "Won't Back Down", there is a feeling of mutual respect at work which puts in perspective Eminem's real attitude towards women despite his Shady misogynistic outbursts. "You can fence in your yard/you can pull all the cards/But I won't back down," cries Pink, with a controlled dignity and strength which sets off nicely against Eminem's typical combative, take-you-all-on waywardness. Some of the lines are not his finest; he fixes on Michael J Fox yet again, "Gotta shake that ass like a Donkey with Parkinson's/Make like Michael J Fox in the jaws playin' with a etch-a-

PINK AT THE 2010 AMERICAN MUSIC AWARDS.

sketch.", cites both Lil and Bruce Wayne, makes fisherman's claims about the length of his penis and, with a typically paradoxical tone of boastful self-deprecation celebrates himself as a "shitstain on the underwear of life" over a thrashing, smackdown metal backbeat.

W.T.P.

One of the funnier, laid-back outings of *Recovery* this, in which Em once again emulates old school bad boy Schoolly D in his vocal stylings. For WTP read White Trash Party and this is rich with details of partytime on the wrong side of the tracks, when both sensibilities and budget are limited.

"Makin' it rain for them ladies in the minis/But I'm not throwin' ones, fives, tens, or even twenties/I'm throwin' quarters, nickels, dimes, pennies up at skinnies." Fuelled with bottles of cheap liquor stuffed down the front of his trousers, Em propositions the ladies thus; "Now hop in my minivan, let's get rowdy!"

GOING THROUGH CHANGES

Here, Eminem revisits some of the autobiographical terrain he was beginning to cover on *Relapse*, but in greater depth and detail. The sample is from Black Sabbath's "Changes" from 1972, a song Ozzy Osbourne later re-made famous when he cut a version of it with his daughter Kelly. As ever, when he feels the heat of the innocent eyes of his own daughters on him, Eminem is at his most repentant and maudlin, much closer to his truer self than the nasty boy who tears around much of the rest of *Recovery*. Amid the sound of smashed mirrors and self-loathing, Eminem reflects on the lows of his drug dependency. "Can see I'm grievin', I try and hide it/But I can't, why do I act like I'm all high and mighty/When inside, I'm dying, I am finally realising I need help/I can't do it by myself, too weak, 2 weeks I've been having ups and downs . . ."

He even allows himself a few lines' reflection on Proof, whose tragic death only helped exacerbate his addiction. But he slaps himself about the face, contrasting his own inertia with the man he felt Proof to be, a man who, he is convinced, would never have been the first to reach for a gun in dispute. "Be a man, stand, a real man woulda had this shit handled/Know you just had your heart ripped out and crushed/They say Proof just flipped out, homie just swift out and bust/Nah, it ain't like Doody to do that/He wouldn't fuckin' shoot at, no-body, he fights first/But dwellin' on it only makes the night worse."

Spitting darts of contempt at the drug pushers who hung around him like flies around a cow's backside, he swats them away and offers a fond lyrical embrace to his daughters and a remarkable assurance about their mother. "Hailie this one is for you, Whitney and Alaina too/I still love your mother, that'll never change/Think about her every day, we just could never get it together." Em may wish he was tougher, the listener might regret the schmaltz of a little girl's voice crying out "Daddy!" over the chorus, but this "soft" side is his human redemption.

NOT AFRAID

This was the first single released from *Recovery*, prior to the album's release, an advance statement of intent. The video for the single sees a non-peroxided Eminem, as if to signal his "4 real-ness", standing on a ledge, at once master of all he surveys, but also on a precipice, from which he draws back. "Not Afraid" is somewhat marred by some trite rhyming ("riding through storms" and "weather, cold or warm"?) and grandiose production and, although Eminem feels a need to set down his mark, he's not 100% in his element when attempting the grand, passionate manner. "Just let you know that, you're not alone/Holla if you feel that you've been down the same road," narrates Em, and you just wonder, if, somewhere in Eminem's divided soul, Slim Shady is sitting on a barstool laughing his skinny ass off at this almost Michael Jackson-like consideration for humanity. "I shoot for the moon/But I'm too busy gazing at stars, I feel amazing," he promises, to which you can only narrow your eyes in hope, rather than assurance. Still, Em is funny as his own best critic, admitting "Let's be honest, that last Relapse CD was 'ehhhh'/Perhaps I ran them accents into the ground/Relax, I ain't going back to that now." These are the sort of lines, the sort of frankness which no other superstar before or since has shown themself to be capable of in song.

SEDUCTION

Over satin sheets of synth strings and almost arabic dollops of Kanye-style autotune, Eminem lays down a sneering, triumphalist snook to every hater, wannabe and schmuck, whose girlfriend would far rather be sharing her bed with Eminem than a loser like them. "There's a seven CD changer in her car/ And I'm in every slot/And you're not." This is one way of Eminem converting his fame into some sort of coinage that the doubters would understand; if he wanted to, he could have any woman he wanted, yours included, homie. "What you expect her to do? How you expect her to act in the sack/When she's closing her eyes, fantasising of digging her nails in my back to this track." Not that it's the sex that Eminem is so much seeking as the confirmation all this represents that "Ain't nobody who's as good at what I do."

NO LOVE

Lil Wayne, one of the rappers Eminem singles out for respect and consideration as a peer and the change in tone and texture he offers after several tracks of verbal pummelling from Em is welcome relief. "Yeah, my life a bitch, but you know nothing bout her/Been to hell and back, I can show you vouchers," drawls Wayne. The word "bitch" features heavily in

the verses and chorus here but it's, "bitch" in the context used here has a broader application than to the female of the species, the way it's used by Jessie in "Breaking Bad"; it's a putdown to any hater, more likely male than female.

The backbeat samples heavily from Haddaway's "What Is Love", again showing Eminem's curious ability to disinter tracks from the '80s/'90s that might otherwise have gone away to die on the sort of night radio stations you only ever hear on cab rides home. The "don't hurt me" line indicates a spasm of vulnerability beneath the rappers' armoury of machismo, a counterpoint to Em-rhymes like "I smell blood, I don't give a fuck, keep giving them hell/Where was you when I fell and needed help up?/You get no love."

In the video for the single release of "No Love", director Chris Robinson manages to extract an anti-bullying fable of sorts for the song; a young lad, picked on in the school toilets, on the basketball court by three bullies, is fired up by listening to Em to round on his aggressors.

LIL WAYNE AT
THE SLEEP TRAIN
AMPHITHEATRE,
CALIFORNIA IN 2011.

SPACE BOUND

Over a cosmically tinged, diaphanous backdrop and
Bowie-esque acoustic strumming, Eminem revisits
once more the central theme of *Recovery*; solitude
on the open road that is the life only you can live.
Again, however, there's a contradiction in some of
Eminem's lines as he works through his emotions.
"Nobody knows me I'm cold/Walk down this road
all alone/It's no one's fault but my own . . . /Frozen
as snow I show no emotion whatsoever so/Don't
ask me why I have no love for these... hos." he
claims to be emotionless and yet expectorates his
lines with the heat of a hundred suns; he takes the
entire blame for his lapses and past predicaments,
which raises the question of why he should have
such animus for the "hos".

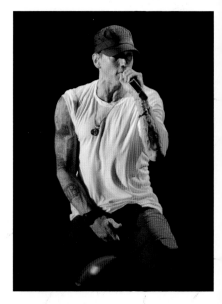

PERFORMING ON
DAY 2 OF THE
V FESTIVAL,
CHELMSFORD,
ENGLAND 2011.

The verses warm up, and Eminem's delivery of
them, as an un-named female, whom he always treated blamelessly,
exasperates him to the point of homicidal rage. "You won't even listen so
fuck it/I'm trying to stop you from breathing/I put both hands on your throat/I
sit on top of you squeezing/Till I snap your neck like a popsicle stick." But it's
Eminem, in the accompanying video in which he appears in dual, split screen
form, who ends up blowing his brains out in sheer, nihilistic frustration.

If there had been praise in some quarters for the positive messages Eminem
was pumping out from his videos at this time, there was criticism for "Space
Bound". He found himself under attack from a British based group, Mothers
Against Violence, who protested that Eminem was using exploitative, bloody
imagery to boost his profile and sales. As to how precisely a music video might
push viewers not already deeply troubled in their own lives into suicide, they
were unforthcoming, as the merchants of moral panic generally are.

CINDERELLA MAN

Even with the mighty Dre at the helm, the instrumental side of Eminem's
work has always been discreet and subordinate, offering a framework for
him to fill in and provide what is essentially the main event, his rapping and

styling and rhyming. Here, however, is an example of a track most striking for its musical content. Lyrically, it's Em flexing his superstar muscles again, smacking down all comers, all those mediocrities who might have stepped into the void had he quit the rap scene. "I shut ya lane down/Took ya spot, parked in it too/Watching it flow, lighter fluid, saliva what can ya do/Go get ya crew to hype you up stand behind you like whoooo!" But it's 25-year-old first timer at the controls Script Shepherd who excels, not just with his mellifluous vocal take on the chorus but also in his piledriving production, the handclapping threatening to break into some mutant variation on Queen's "We Will Rock You".

It's a stadium feel, an anthem," Shepherd told MTV. "Like marching, marching towards something. The sound is big, the message is big on the record. It's about just coming from nothing, not doubting yourself. It sounds like you're marching towards a goal. The guitars are rifting, and it has little bells keeping it melodic. It's a strong record that's motivating. And Em did something motivating with it. I just wanted to have people feel like they're moving with the record, have a 'Rocky' feel. It sounded more authentic to have people feel like they were stomping in the record."

25 TO LIFE

Working around a twitchy synth accompaniment that matches Eminem's trembling rage, this is yet another take on his fraught attachment to Kim, which he compares to a prison sentence. Railing against her for failing to understand the sacrifices he's made for her and his continued fidelity, he attempts to assert himself as the 800 pound, breast beating, dominant male. "Imma take control of this relationship/Command it/And I'm gonna be the boss of you now goddammit/And what I mean is that/I'm will no longer let you control me."

However, even as the verses progress, even as he tries to be Superman, it's clear that Kim is his Kryptonite. Who's he kidding? He can't help himself. "Got a special place for you/In my heart/That I have kept/It's unfortunate but it's too late/For the other side/Caught in a chase/25 to life." Somehow, as if in a dream sequence, hip-hop himself becomes his mistress. In the final verse threatens to quit that too, but he's no more capable of doing that than he is banishing Kim from his life.

SO BAD

Sometimes Eminem is accused of poorly sequencing his album tracks but this sits ironically well after "25 To Life", with Em escaping into his shady persona, as he puts out all his wildest and sleaziest lines to a female enticed into his Mercedes. "Girl don't be so frantic I'm just a hopeless romantic,/ Don't try to fight the feeling of something that's organic," he pleads, though then goes on to rather ruin the Romeo effect. "You can't ignore it, so don't just stand before it/Just drop them panties to the floor, let's get to camcording." Typically self-analytically, Eminem reflects on his own Dad. "I must have got my pimping genes from him, the way he left my mama/I'm a rolling stone just like him," but of course, the truth is that, unlike his own father, the last thing Eminem would ever do, for all the vicissitudes in his life and marriage, is walk away from his children.

ALMOST FAMOUS

Another of Eminem's warnings to the would-be celebrity seeker to be careful of what they wish for. In fairness, Eminem himself never actively sought or visualised the level of fame he would achieve; his stated intention, very early on, was simply to "get by" as a rapper. Although he thrives on the notion of being at the absolute top of his game, all-conquering and peerless, he is fully aware that the more spiritually eviscerating aspects of celebrity life would make mere unconditioned mortals quail. He's had to become very good at it. "Wake up behind these trenches, you run around defenceless/There is too much to lose/You cannot fill these shoes".

In the verses, Em reaches deep into his grab-bag of tastelessness, as if to demonstrate what it takes to fill said shoes; "Don't call me the champ, call me the space shuttle destroyer/I just blew up the challenger, matter of fact, I need a lawyer/I just laced my gloves with enough plaster to make a cast/Beat his ass naked and peed in his corner like Verne Troyer," he spits, in reference to the "Mini-Me" actor who was embroiled in a sex tape scandal involving his former girlfriend. The mysterious death of the actor David Carradine, possibly through autoerotic misadventure (he was found hanged in a closet in a Bangkok hotel room) is also alluded to as he smacks down the naysayers; "Like David Carradine, they can go fuck themselves and just die."

LOVE THE WAY YOU LIE

One of the most controversial tracks, this, not for any outrageous or provocative lyrical content but because of the good it purported to do. Having been assaulted by her own boyfriend, singer Chris Brown, prior to the Grammy Awards in February 2009 (for which Brown was sentenced to 180 days' community labour, five years' probation and unending shame), R&B star Rihanna declared that the video she made with Eminem for "Love The Way You Lie" was intended to raise consciousness about the dangers of domestic violence.

Certainly, Eminem is in fine, frank and self-excoriating mood on this single, as he guiltily relives some of the exchanges he has had with Kim in his time, and moments of jealousy. He even confesses to laying hands on Kim. "I'll never stoop so low again . . . I guess I don't know my own strength." He later promises to plant his fist "in a dry wall" should he experience further violent feelings. In reality, no one knows for certain if Eminem was habitually physically abusive to Kim, or if there are instances of the sort which have had such a devastating effect on Chris Brown's career and reputation. The reality may be closer to what transpires in the actual video, which, critics have argued, does not really address the squalid, one-sided reality of domestic violence at all.

As Rihanna rolls out the sultry chorus and Eminem pumps out the verses, striding, buff and photogenic, through a wheat field, we see actors Megan Fox and Dominic Monaghan (of *Lost* fame) lying in bed together in a sexy tableau. However, theirs is clearly a volatile relationship in which each gives just about as good as they get, and whose violence generally seems to be a form of vigorous foreplay, a prelude to make-up sex. At the end, although their house is in flames, this is in keeping with their grand passion, rather than a domestic disaster.

Said Rihanna to *Access Hollywood*: "It just was authentic. It was real. It was believable for us to do a record like that, but it was also something that needed to be done. He (Eminem) pretty much just broke down the cycle of domestic violence and it touches a lot of people." She later told *Billboard*, "The clip aims at highlighting the dangers of an abusive relationship and, indirectly, delivers the

EMINEM AND RIHANNA AT THE V FESTIVAL IN 2011.

169

message that it's better to walk out before it's too late." Certainly, it marked a shift towards PC acceptability for Eminem the supposed misogynist, who at this time also voiced his approval for gay marriage, on the grounds that in his view, everyone had the right to be equally miserable!

YOU'RE NEVER OVER

A misty, scathing cascade of metal guitar, bullet-like percussion and a distant choir chanting the chorus like a heavenly host (sampled from Gerard McMann's "Cry Little Sister") all of these are indicators that Eminem was looking to pull out all the stops for this, effectively the album's closer. It's his belated address to his late mentor Proof, or at least his spirit, to whom Eminem both pays tribute and draws strength from. All of the themes of *Recovery* are pulled together in this final outing – the loneliness of life at the top, the assorted "bitches", real and imagined who have bedevilled his comeback and his determination to rise again, cleansed and with his appetite for creative destruction renewed. "For you, I wanna write the sickest rhyme of my life/So sick it'll blow up the mic . . ."

So there it is. Only a passing reference to Mike Tyson is jarringly dated; the boxer was a pitiful shell of his former self at this time, but otherwise, Em is rapping up a storm, all talk of retirement out of the window, his energies redoubled rather than diminished by the passing of his old friend. "Instead of mourning your death, I'd rather celebrate your life/Elevate to new height...".

EMINEM PERFORMS WITH DR DRE AT THE 53RD GRAMMY AWARDS.

UNTITLED

… except that's not quite the end. "I ain't finished yet," smirks Eminem, over a swingalong backbeat strangely akin to "What's New, Pussycat?" and delivers one of the most technically immaculate, toxically obnoxious lyrics – Eminem at his best, doing his worst.

**BUN B AND ROYCE
DA 5'9" AT THE
HIGHLINE BALLROOM
IN 2011**

RIDAZ

The first of two tracks featured on the Deluxe edition, "Ridaz" is a fabulous Dre production, recalling some of the tanned, low-riding swagger of "California", with the title cascading in looping stages throughout. Lyrically, it's Eminem in barroom smackdown mode, delivering his adversaries the sort of elaborate, sustained, verbal pistol-whipping most of us would like to mete out when crossed.

SESSION ONE

Another more stripped-down production, a crush of organs, metal guitar and trad drumkit in simulated live concert conditions, Em is joined here by Slaughterhouse, with Royce Da 5'9", Joell Ortiz and Crooked I adding verses in tandem with Em himself, having fun as if in encore mode, cooked and relaxed, in full, (self) celebratory flow. No one upstages, or is upstaged; this is Eminem, whose caucasian-ness has never prevented him from being one of the most assured and belonging members of the rap community.

DISCOGRAPHY

ALBUMS

Infinite
(1996, Web Entertainment)

The Slim Shady LP
(1999, Aftermath/Interscope)

The Marshall Mathers LP
(2000, Aftermath/Interscope)

The Eminem Show
(2002, Aftermath/Interscope)

Encore
(2004, Aftermath/Interscope)

Curtain Call: The Hits
(2006, Shady/Aftermath/Interscope)

Relapse
(2009, Aftermath/Interscope)

Recovery
(2010, Shady/Aftermath/Interscope)

ALBUMS (WITH D12)

The Underground EP
(1997, Bass Brothers)

Devil's Night
(2001, Shady/Interscope)

D12 World
(2004, Shady/Interscope)

SINGLES/EPS

The Slim Shady EP
(1998, Web Entertainment)

AS EMINEM:

Just Don't Give a Fuck/Brain Damage
(1998, Aftermath/Interscope)

My name Is
(1998, Aftermath/Interscope)

Any Man
(1999, Rawkus)

Guilty Conscience
(1999, Aftermath/Interscope)

The Real Slim Shady
(2000, Aftermath/Interscope)

The Way I Am/Bad Influence
(2000, Aftermath/Interscope)

Stan
(2000, Aftermath/Interscope)

Without Me
(2002, Shady/Aftermath/Interscope)

Cleaning Out My Closet
(2002, Shady/Aftermath/Interscope)

Lose Yourself
(2002, Shady/Aftermath/Interscope)

Superman
(2003, Shady/Aftermath/Interscope)

Sing For The Moment
(2003, Shady/Aftermath/Interscope)

Business
(2003, Shady/Aftermath/Interscope)

Just Lose It
(2004, Shady/Aftermath/Interscope)

Encore
(2004, Shady/Aftermath/Interscope)

Like Toy Soldiers
(2005, Shady/Aftermath/Interscope)

Mockingbird
(2005, Shady/Aftermath/Interscope)

Ass Like That
(2005, Shady/Aftermath/Interscope)

Eminem
(2005, Shady/Aftermath/Interscope)

When I'm Gone
(2005, Shady/Aftermath/Interscope)

Shake That (featuring Nate Dogg)
(2006 Shady/Aftermath/Interscope)

You Don't Know
(with 50 Cent, Lloyd Banks and Cashis)

Jimmy Crack Corn (with 50 Cent)

**Crack a Bottle
(featuring Dr. Dre and 50 Cent)**
(2009, Shady/Aftermath/Interscope)

We Made You
(2009, Shady/Aftermath/Interscope)

3 a.m.
(2009, Shady/Aftermath/Interscope)

Old Time's Sake (featuring Dr. Dre)
(2009, Shady/Aftermath/Interscope)

Beautiful
(2009, Shady/Aftermath/Interscope)

Hell Breaks Loose
(2009, Shady/Aftermath/Interscope)

Elevator
(2009, Shady/Aftermath/Interscope)

Not Afraid
(2010, Shady/Aftermath/Interscope)

Love the Way You Lie (featuring Rihanna)
(2010, Shady/Aftermath/Interscope)

No Love (featuring Lil Wayne)
(2010, Shady/Aftermath/Interscope)

Space Bound
(2011, Shady/Aftermath/Interscope)

SOUNDTRACK APPEARANCES

Bad Guys Always Die, featuring Dr Dre
(Wild Wild West soundtrack. 1999. Interscope)

Off The Wall, featuring Redman
(The Nutty Professor II: The Klumps soundtrack. 2000. Def Jam)

Lose Yourself
(8 Mile soundtrack, 2002, Shady/Interscope)

Love Me, featuring Obie Trice and 50 Cent
(8 Mile soundtrack, 2002, Shady/Interscope)

8 Mile
(8 Mile soundtrack, 2002, Shady/Interscope)

Rabbit Run
(8 Mile soundtrack, 2002, Shady/Interscope)

Stimulate
(8 Mile soundtrack, 2002, Shady/Interscope)

Go To Sleep, featuring Obie Trice and DMX
(Cradle 2 The Grave soundtrack, 2003, Def Jam)

COLLABORATIONS

1996

Fuckin' Backstabber/Biterphobia (With Soul Intent)

1998

Trife Thieves (with Bizarre, Fuzz Scoota)

We Shine (with Da Ruckus)

Fuck off (with Kid Rock)

Green and Gold (with The Anonymous)

1999

Hustlers & Hardcore (with Feel-X)

The Anthem (with Chino XL, Kool G Rap, KRS-One, Jayo Felony, Pharoahe Monch, RZA, Sway & King Tech, Tech N9ne, Xzibit)

Get You Mad (with Sway & King Tech)

Bad Guys Always Die (with Dr. Dre)

Busa Rhyme (with Missy Elliott)

The Last Hit (with The High & Mighty)

Stir Crazy (with The Madd Rapper)

Bad Influence (with Dr Dre)

What's the Difference (with Dr. Dre, Xzibit)

Forgot About Dre (with Dr. Dre)

Murder, Murder (Remix) (with Twiztid)

Dead Wrong (with The Notorious B.I.G)

If I Get Locked Up (with Dr. Dre)

2000

Rush Ya Clique (with Outsidaz)

Watch Deez (with Thirstin Howl III)

Get Back (with D12)

Hellabound (H&H Remix) (with J Black, Maste Ase)

3 6 5 (with Skam)

Off the Wall (with Redman)

Desperados (with Proof, Bugz)

What If I Was White (with Sticky Fingaz)

Words Are Weapons (with D12)

Don't Approach Me (with Xzibit)

What the Beat (with Royce Da 5'9", Method Man)

2001

Renegade (with Jay-Z)

2002

My Name (with Xzibit, Nate Dogg)

Rock City (with Royce Da 5'9")

2003

Patiently Waiting (with 50 Cent)

Don't Push Me (with 50 Cent, Lloyd Banks)

Go to Sleep (with DMX, Obie Trice)

Lady (Obie Trice)

Shit Hits the Fan (with Dr. Dre, Obie Trice)

We All Die One Day
(with 50 Cent, Obie Trice, Lloyd Banks, Tony Yayo)

Hands on You (with Obie Trice)

Outro (with D12, Obie Trice)

911 (with Boo-Yaa T.R.I.B.E., B-Real)

One Day at a Time (Em's Version) (with 2Pac, Outlawz)

Freestyle (with DJ Kayslay)

2004

I'm Gone (with Obie Trice)

Welcome to D-Block (with D-Block)

Warrior, Pt. 2 (with 50 Cent, Lloyd Banks, Nate Dogg)

Soldier Like Me (with 2Pac)

Black Cotton (with 2Pac, Kastro, Young Noble)

2005

We Ain't (with The Game)

Gatman and Robbin (with 50 Cent)

My Ballz (with D12)

Lean Back (Remix) (with Fat Joe, Lil Jon, Remy Ma)

Hip Hop (with Bizarre)

Drama Setter (with Obie Trice, Tony Yayo)

Pimplikeness (with D12)

Off to Tijuana (with D12, Hush)

It Has Been Said (with Notorious B.I.G., Obie Trice, Diddy)

Welcome 2 Detroit (with Trick-Trick)

No More to Say (with Proof, Trick-Trick)

2006

I'll Hurt You (with Busta Rhymes)

There They Go (with Obie Trice, Big Herk)

Smack That (with Akon)

Eminem Presents: The Re-Up LP (with Obie Trice, Stat Quo, Bobby Creekwater, Cashis, Bizarre, Kuniva, Lloyd Banks, Swifty McVay, Denaun Porter, Akon)

2007

Pistol Poppin' (with Cashis)

Touchdown (with T.I.)

Peep Show (with 50 Cent)

2008

Who Want It (with Trick-Trick)

2009

Chemical Warfare (with The Alchemist)

Forever (with Drake, Kanye West, Lil Wayne)

Psycho (with 50 Cent)

2010

Drop the World (with Lil Wayne)

Airplanes, Part II (with B.o.B, Hayley Williams)

Love the Way You Lie (Part II) (with Rihanna)

Roman's Revenge (with Nicki Minaj)

Celebrity (with Lloyd Banks, Akon)

Where I'm At (with Lloyd Banks)

That's All She Wrote (with T.I.)

2011

I Need a Doctor (with Dr. Dre, Skylar Grey)

Writer's Block (with Royce da 5'9")

Never Be The Same (with Young Jeezy)

Hell: The Sequel EP (as Bad Meets Evil)

INDEX